DATE DUE

DE 1 1 99			

Technical Services
in the
Medium-Sized Library

Technical Services in the Medium-Sized Library

An Investigation of Current Practices

Sheila S. Intner

and

Josephine Riss Fang

with a Foreword by Robert D. Stueart

Library Professional Publications 1991

Copyright 1991 by Sheila S. Intner and Josephine Riss Fang
All rights reserved.
Published 1991 as a Library Professional Publication,
an imprint of The Shoe String Press, Inc.,
Hamden, Connecticut 06514

Printed in the United States of America

Library of Congress Cataloging-in-Publication data:

Intner, Sheila S.
Technical services in the medium-sized
library : an investigation of current practices
Sheila S. Intner and Josephine Riss Fang.
p.   cm.
Includes bibliographical references (p. 181) and index.
1. Processing (Libraries)
2. Processing (Libraries)—Automation.
I. Fang, Josephine R. II. Title.
Z688.5.I58   91-18311   025.02—dc20
ISBN 0-208-02173-6

Contents

Foreword by Robert D. Stueart   vii

Preface   ix

Introduction   xi

1. The Setting   1

2. Computing in Technical Services   10

3. Acquisitions and Collection Management   35

4. Preservation Management   60

5. Cataloging, Classification, and Indexing   73

6. Document Delivery: Circulation Control and Interlibrary Loan   97

7. Coordinated Collection Development   123

8. Beyond the Nineties: Electronic Libraries and Technical Services   139
    Pamela Reekes McKirdy

Appendix: The Survey: List of Participating Institutions and Survey Instrument   159

Glossary of Acronyms and Selected Terms   161

Notes   171

Selected Annotated Bibliography   181

Index   185

Foreword

There has been a great deal of discussion recently—in conference corridors and in the literature—about technical services. Speculation has ranged from the problems of a shortage of catalogers to decentralization of what was once known as the technical processes in libraries; from discussions about the Library of Congress and its role in centralized cataloging to the traditional stand-off between "those people in technical services" as opposed to those in public services. The debate continues. Many questions continue to surface from it.

This volume was conceived to answer some of the questions. It not only describes current technical services operations, but also speaks to the issues identified by technical services staff.

The authors of this treatise are well qualified to address the issues. Dr. Sheila S. Intner has made substantial contributions to the development of technical services through her monographic and serial writings, through editing *Library Resources & Technical Services*, through consulting in all types of libraries, and through her teaching. Dr. Josephine Riss Fang also has been active, particularly in the areas of preservation issues, acquisitions, and publishing.

This work builds on the philosophies and processes first eloquently described by Maurice Tauber.

Robert D. Stueart
  Dean, Graduate School of Library and Information Science
  Simmons College
  Boston, Massachusetts

Preface

This book describes current thinking about the organization and functioning of technical service departments in general and provides a brief look at technical service operations reported by a small group of medium-sized academic and public libraries in the United States. It is intended for library managers—particularly if their institutions match the profile of libraries studied for this book—who should keep abreast of activities and trends in these essential services; for library school educators and students who study technical service functions and operations; and for practicing librarians—those in the technical service department, whose knowledge might benefit from collegial sharing, and those in public service departments, whose understanding of the challenges their colleagues face could help them work together more effectively.

The descriptions in this book are based on current activities reported by the librarians who participated in the survey, by hundreds of practitioners who have spoken with us at seminars, meetings, and workshops, and by our observations of technical service operations in libraries for whom we have consulted.

The survey libraries were a group of 120 medium-sized libraries, selected from the *American Library Directory*. "Medium-sized" was defined as college and university libraries serving student populations between 2,500 and 10,000 and public libraries serving populations between 50,000 and 150,000. We are grateful to all the respondents, both those who chose to remain anonymous and the twenty-eight who allowed their names to be revealed. Their comments are quoted throughout the text, affording a variety of snapshot views from real librarians working under all the budgetary, environmental, and managerial constraints that pervade the real world of practice.

We also wish to thank the Graduate School of Library and Information Science, Simmons College, and the Emily Hollowell Research Fund for providing the generous support that made the survey and subsequent data analyses possible.

A large measure of appreciation is due to Linda Watkins, Simmons College library science librarian, whose expert assistance and advice throughout the project was invaluable. As always, faculty secretary Linda Willey and her student assistants helped in many ways during each step of the research and writing process, which contributed enormously to its progress. They all have our thanks.

Finally, we wish to extend our gratitude to Virginia H. Mathews of The Shoe String Press, who initiated the idea that became *Technical Services in the Medium-Sized Library*, and who shepherded it through the many agonies of writing, editing, and transforming it into a finished book.

Introduction

This book is devoted to a description and analysis of technical services in libraries, especially medium-sized public and academic libraries. To begin at the beginning, it is useful to ask some questions: What are technical services in libraries? Why are they called "technical?" Is there more than one acceptable definition for the phrase? If so, what are the boundaries of these definitions?

A Working Definition of Technical Services

What are technical services in libraries?

Technical services usually are thought of as that set of activities performed behind the scenes, without direct contact with the library's public, by which library materials are acquired and organized for use. Historically, the two functions of acquisition and cataloging were considered central to technical services. But this simple definition of technical services began expanding as early as the 1950s when Maurice Tauber said, in his seminal work, *Technical Services in Libraries*:

> In most modern libraries . . . many of the library personnel are not known to the clientele. These are the order or acquisition librarians, the catalogers and classifiers, the binding librarians, the photographic assistants, and certain members of the circu-

lation staff. These are not all the personnel who work behind the scenes, away from the service desks, but, primarily, they are the ones who perform *the technical work of acquiring, recording, preserving, and circulating materials* for the use of patrons.[1] (Emphasis added.)

In 1984, editor Irene P. Godden wrote in *Library Technical Services*:

> The present text is therefore intended to give an overview of current operations and techniques associated with the acquisition, organization for access, and physical processing and maintenance of collections of library materials.[2]

Godden and her associates included chapters in their book about the specific functions of acquisitions, bibliographic control, preservation and materials processing, and circulation functions, in addition to general chapters about technical services administration and automation.

Even more recently, in 1990, Michael Gorman wrote in *Technical Services Today and Tomorrow*:

> The broad definition of technical services that informs this book is as follows: All the tasks carried on in a library that are concerned with the processing of library materials in order to make them accessible to the users of the library. Such processes include:
>
> • ordering, claiming, and receipt of library materials
> • cataloguing and classification
> • serials control
> • database and catalogue maintenance
> • marking of processed materials
> • shelving and retrieval
> • circulation (charging and discharging)
> • binding and preservation
> • collection management
> • budgeting and planning for these activities
>
> It may be helpful for the purposes of definition to state briefly the tasks carried out by library professionals that are *not* comprehended by this definition. Broadly speaking they are:
>
> • selection of library materials
> • collection development

- reference and other user services
- instruction in the use of the library.[3]

Why are these activities called "technical?"

According to Tauber, the application of techniques amenable to codification distinguished the technical services from those of the public service desk. He said:

> The use of the term *technical services*, or any of its variants (*technical operations, technical activities*, or *technical processes*), is comparatively recent in library terminology. . . . The use of the term *technical*, however, does denote that certain operations which are usually carried on away from the public desks are likely to be more susceptible to codification than those of the readers' departments. Some of the operations of the circulation and reference departments are also "technical" in this sense and are therefore considered in this volume.[4] (Emphasis in the original.)

Tauber might be surprised to discover that, almost forty years later, some of the activities of the public service desk have been codified too—especially appropriate methods of searching online databases to answer patron queries and, even, how to conduct reference interviews. Thus the application of formal techniques to work is no longer a rationale for dividing technical and public service activities.

It is more useful to fall back on the fundamental principle that the performance of a librarian's job responsibilities without any interaction with the public is the distinguishing feature of technical services. Technical activities focus on materials rather than on the people who use them. They have become synonymous with materials preparation, processing, maintenance, and preservation, and the management of all of these services.

Even this definition is not absolute, however, since some technical service activities might include assisting or consulting with the people who use catalogs and other bibliographic control files, especially after these are computerized. The technical service staff member has become a resource person, not only for the staff user, but for the end user as well. In addition, some libraries are beginning to rethink the organizational divisions into public and technical service specialties, hiring librarians with the understanding that they will have responsibilities in both areas.[5] These dual role assignments take advantage of subject and language expertise for selection and cataloging tasks as well as for reference work; they obviate the need to duplicate the same expertise for two departments. Dual role librarians also appear to function well in a computerized environment in which a central bibliographic database serves all library service areas, not just the public service areas or the technical service areas.

Is there more than one acceptable definition for the phrase "technical services?"

Libraries with technical service departments or divisions subsume different operations under them, so one could say that definitions differ based on actual practice. Even the core activities of acquisition and cataloging are apportioned to different departments in some institutions, e.g., in some libraries, acquisition means book purchasing, but not serial and periodical purchasing or the acquisition of government documents. These are assigned instead to the reference department or to separate serials and documents departments that report to a public service administrator. Indeed, the cataloging of audiovisual materials, government documents, and children's materials are sometimes given to the audiovisual, document, and children's departments respectively, not to the cataloging department under the technical services umbrella.

What are the boundaries of these definitions?

Definitional boundaries most often are based on local perceptions of the proper place of services for special types of materials (serials, periodicals, audiovisuals, government documents) or materials for special audiences (such as children and youth, people with impaired vision, or non-English speakers).

They also may differ based on local perceptions of the scope of individual services themselves. Acquisition of materials always includes placing orders, monitoring receipt of materials, and paying for them. In a growing number of libraries, however, acquisition means all the activities of collection development and management as well, such as planning for future needs, allocating funds among departments, selecting desired titles, evaluating collections, and monitoring the continued physical wellbeing of materials after they are acquired. This last-named responsibility is sometimes termed "collection maintenance" and includes management of shelving operations; it could be called "preservation" and include direction of binding and repair facilities and microfilming activities. It could include them all.

Cataloging—also called "processing," "organization," or "bibliographic control"—most often includes all the processes of creating and maintaining cataloging records for acquired materials and classifying them for arrangement on library shelves. It sometimes includes the tasks of maintaining all bibliographic files, including those of the order department(s), circulation department, and interlibrary loan department. It also may include other non-bibliographic processing activities such as barcoding items for circulation, or stamping, covering, marking, or otherwise making them identifiable as library materials and readying them for shelving and use.

The boundaries of technical services depend on perceptions of what is appropriately "technical" and of who is the logical focus of leadership for particular activities. Only activities that involve direct interaction with the public, such as checking out books, answering questions, or giving instruction in the use of the library, are excluded routinely from technical services in virtually all libraries.

Purposes of This Study

THE LIBRARIES STUDIED

The study on which this book is based was undertaken to determine current organizational and operational characteristics of technical service departments in medium-sized academic and public libraries. Researchers often study and report on the administrative organization and operational activities of the very largest libraries, particularly that group of large research libraries distinguished by membership in the Association of Research Libraries (ARL). ARL's Office of Management Services provides a base for such studies and publishes the results for the benefit of all who are interested. Librarians practicing in ARL libraries may be encouraged (some might say "prodded") to conduct research studies as part of their job responsibilities in much the same way that academic faculties are required to "publish or perish" in order to attain promotion and tenure or to qualify for salary increases. Tauber's study, too, was based primarily on activities observed in general research libraries, which tend to be relatively large and which require that areas of specialization be defined within the organizational structure. Tauber cautioned:

> While it is hoped that [*Technical Services in Libraries*] will be of interest to librarians in various types of libraries, many of the problems discussed in it are related principally to the research library. Moreover, certain types of libraries—law libraries, medical libraries, and other kinds of special libraries—have special technical problems or problems involving control of materials which are not treated in detail in this volume. School libraries, many public libraries which are not particularly concerned with research, and some college libraries are likely to simplify some of the operations described.[6]

Gorman, whose book is, he writes, "not for the absolute beginner," also states that "the majority of contributors to this book have an academic/research library background. In one or two instances . . . the discussion is largely or wholly devoted to academic/research library concerns. In the other chapters, a conscious effort has been made to generalize the topic and, thus, make it interesting and relevant to the reader no matter what her or his library background may be."[7]

Indeed, far less attention seems to be paid to smaller institutions, even though there are many more of them. Medium-sized libraries—whether academic or public—have no organization comparable to ARL to sponsor and fund research on their behalf. Librarians practicing in medium-sized libraries appear to publish fewer articles than their peers in larger libraries, although this was not tested empirically and might be merely a misperception. In any case, we were interested in investigating the status of technical services in medium-sized academic and public libraries, because such information is not common knowledge, despite the fact that the group of libraries comprising this group accounts for a large segment of professional practice.

THE IMPACT OF AUTOMATION

We were interested, too, in exploring the thesis that computer-based systems, available and affordable for nearly twenty years at the time of this writing, have become an integral part of contemporary technical service departments. We also wished to test the notion that the organization and functioning of the departments have changed in profound ways, suggesting that the paradigm described by Maurice Tauber and his associates at Columbia University in the early 1950s might no longer be reflected in the workflow, tasks, staffing, and structure of contemporary libraries, but instead may have been replaced by a new organizational structure incorporating the use of computer-based bibliographic databases.

THE DEMISE OF TECHNICAL SERVICES

If the literature of library and information science can be believed, technical service departments are shrinking to the point of disappearing. This is said to be a result of automation. Three things are alleged to have happened:

• the spread of bibliographic networks and local automated systems caused a dramatic decline in the size of cataloging units;
• acquisitions units were broadened into collection development and management units, and merged into public service departments;

• technical services were subsumed under new organizational divisions called "automated systems," "computer services," or some variation on those themes.

Job advertisements, however, present quite a different picture. These indicate that many libraries actively seek technical service librarians.

Library educators and managers were so deeply troubled about shortages of candidates for technical service positions that two committees were formed in the 1980s to study the problem. One was the American Library Association/Resources and Technical Services Division/Cataloging and Classification Section ad hoc Task Force on Recruiting and Education for Cataloging (the division known as RTSD until June of 1989 is now named the Association for Library Collections and Technical Services, or ALCTS). Established in 1986, this group became a standing committee within the Cataloging and Classification Section of RTSD in 1988. The second committee, sponsored by the Association for Library and Information Science Education (ALISE), was the Special Interest Group on Technical Services Education, established in 1987. Both groups were trying to determine the extent of the problems, focus attention on them, identify potential solutions, and promote their implementation.[8] In the spring of 1989, with funding from the Council on Library Resources, the Graduate School of Library and Information Science of Simmons College sponsored a symposium in which thirty speakers offered solutions to the threefold problems of recruiting, educating, and training catalogers. The symposium attracted an audience of 100 concerned librarians from the U.S., Canada, and Europe, who listened and participated in the discussions that followed the formal presentations.[9]

A study profiling contemporary technical service departments seemed to be the only way to distinguish fact from supposition and current realities from forecasts that may or may not have come to pass. As this book is being written, the twenty-first century is just a few years away. It seems to be the right time to ask if prognostications made in the 1960s and 1970s for a future that is now the recent past actually happened, and to reassess current trends in technical service management in order to make new forecasts for the next decade and the new millenium.

Population of the Study

We decided to examine technical services operations in medium-sized public and academic libraries because there are so many of them and because their problems may be overlooked in serious research. Also, medium-sized libraries were developed as a market by automation vendors years before their larger colleagues. What responses to automation might have emerged in these libraries?

Observers may be correct in believing that the actions of large research libraries frequently influence the rest of the information community far beyond their numbers, but their automation activities have been extremely uneven. Some large research libraries, e.g., the Library of Congress, Northwestern University, Stanford University, Ohio State University, and the University of Chicago, pioneered in automation research and development with mainframe computers long before mini- and microcomputers arrived on the scene. Other large libraries deferred their plans until late in the 1970s. Perhaps this was because the enormous task of converting their catalogs to machine-readable form was so daunting, or perhaps they were unwilling or unable to make the financial commitments necessary to implement the new technologies on the scale required by their large number of staff members, holdings, and users.

Whatever the reasons, medium-sized libraries were able to take advantage of the introduction of minicomputer-based turnkey systems, beginning in 1970, with CLSI's LIBS 100 circulation control system. CLSI quickly was joined by other firms anxious to serve libraries' automation needs, bringing healthy competition in their wake. Computing research and development progressed at a dizzying rate throughout the 1970s, with hardware becoming smaller in size and less costly, but larger in storage capacity and more powerful. In

1980, microcomputer-based systems entered the marketplace, bringing computing within reach of virtually all libraries. It would seem that, having smaller collections and the greater flexibility of smaller size, medium-sized libraries should have been able to adopt computer technology more quickly than their larger colleagues and, therefore, already have experienced whatever ancillary changes automation might bring. Or, so we hypothesized at the start of the study.

For this study, 120 academic and public libraries were selected from the *American Library Directory*.[10] The academic libraries are located in colleges and universities having student populations of no fewer than 2,500 and no more than 10,000. The public libraries serve municipalities of no fewer than 50,000 and no more than 150,000 inhabitants. Libraries located in all parts of the United States are represented among the respondents. Some of the public libraries are, more precisely, library systems consisting of a central library and branches, or several co-equal agencies. Such systems were considered one unit. In the same way, the library system of a single academic institution was considered one library for the purposes of the study, even though it might consist of several departments, buildings, or branches at different locations.

A total of sixty-one usable responses were received. Respondents could choose to be identified or remain anonymous. Twenty-eight of them chose to divulge their identities: thirteen public and fifteen academic libraries (see Appendix). Follow-up interviews by telephone were conducted with some of the identified librarians to clarify or elaborate on their written answers. This book was based on the written and oral information provided through these questionnaires and interviews.

Methodology of the Study

A questionnaire surveying the organization, staffing, and operations of the technical service department was mailed to the designated libraries. (A sample questionnaire appears in the appendix.) The questionnaire was divided into nine sections, beginning with general information about the library and the technical service department as a whole, progressing through the individual functions of acquisitions, serials control, cataloging and classification, processing, binding and preservation, circulation control, and collection management, and concluding with a section on computer systems.

The survey requested purely descriptive information, but even these relatively simple descriptions are not entirely comparable. Every question allowed for unusual responses and each section asked for an open-ended description of aspects the librarians believed to be unique. Even the names applied to the unit differed, with some of them called technical services while others are called processing or support services.[11] Thus, the frequency with which an answer was selected was less important than the total profile that emerged for each institution. Descriptive statistics were employed to the extent they could be useful, but when responses diverged to the point that they were no longer comparable, no attempt was made to draw conclusions based on the frequency of responses.

The book begins with brief descriptions of the settings in which the surveyed libraries exist, followed by a general examination of popular manual and automated systems that perform technical services functions. Subsequent chapters describe each functional area within technical services. They follow the order of the survey, which roughly parallels the stages through which materials pass in their progress through the library: acquisitions and collection management; cataloging and classification; document delivery; coordinated collection development, which impacts both on document delivery and acquisitions and collection management; and preservation management. The final chapter, by Pamela Reekes McKirdy, formerly a member of the Simmons College faculty specializing in systems analysis and automated systems and services, speculates on what trends might be anticipated for the future.

— 1 —

The Setting

What kinds of libraries are "medium-sized?" What kinds of municipalities were surveyed? What sorts of colleges and universities fit within the parameters outlined in the Introduction? A brief look at the libraries and librarians included in the survey population of 120 libraries seems in order as well as a profile of the respondents, their positions, and their departments within the library organization.[1]

The Survey Population

MEDIUM-SIZED ACADEMIC INSTITUTIONS

Sixty academic institutions offering at least a four-year undergraduate program were selected for the survey.[2] Forty of these institutions included the word "university" in their names. Of the rest, seventeen called themselves colleges and the balance used the term "institute." State university branches in Alabama, Arkansas, California, Colorado, Connecticut, Indiana, Kentucky, Louisiana, Maryland, Mississippi, New Mexico, North Dakota, Ohio, Oklahoma, Oregon, South Dakota, Texas, Washington, and Wisconsin were among them. As one might imagine, the state university libraries included here represented the smaller institutions in states such as California, Connecticut, Ohio, Texas, and Wisconsin.

Twenty-five of the colleges and universities were located in urban settings, such as Augusta (Georgia), Baltimore, Boston, Bridgeport, Chicago, Dallas, Fort Worth, Kansas City (Missouri), New York, Providence, St. Louis, San Francisco, South Bend (Indiana), and Tallahassee. Sixteen institutions were located in the northeastern United States; nineteen were located in sunbelt states; ten were located in the far west; and fifteen in the central states.

Most of the participating libraries were in institutions offering general academic programs; five identified themselves as specializing in science and/or technology. Two colleges had Christian religious affiliations. One institution offered the degree of "educational specialist" as its highest degree; five gave the baccalaureate as the highest degree; twenty-five gave a master's degree; and the others listed the doctor of philosophy as the highest degree granted.

Student populations ranged from 2,070 at the smallest campus to 10,000 at the largest. Thirty-five institutions had student populations between 2,000 and 5,000; eighteen had between 5,000 and 7,500 students; and seven had between 7,500 and 10,000 students. Faculties varied in number from 120 to 1,138 members, but the way they were counted was not specified. There was no way of knowing whether solely full-time faculty were counted; whether full-time, part-time, adjuncts, and lecturers were counted equally; or whether the total represented an adjusted figure for full-time equivalents. Also, there was no way to know if librarians and administrators with faculty status were counted with the teaching faculty.

Faculty-student ratios (based on reported figures) varied from 3:1 to 47:1. One might expect institutions giving Ph.D.s to have lower student-faculty ratios than those giving only baccalaureates. This was true for the 120 institutions selected for this study, with those granting Ph.D.s having the lowest average ratio among the three groups: eighteen students for each faculty member. However, institutions which gave master's degrees had the highest average student-faculty ratio—24:1—while those granting bachelor's degrees averaged 21:1.

Reported holdings of books in these libraries varied from

49,100 volumes to 2,169,792, but the higher figure included bound volumes of periodicals. Only three other libraries reported book holdings of more than 1,000,000 volumes; none of these specified including anything other than monographs. It is very difficult to ascertain exactly what is counted, with some institutions listing volumes, others titles, some giving both titles and volumes, and some including anything bound between covers (e.g., documents, periodicals, other serials). Periodical subscriptions ranged from a low of 621 (in a library holding 92,044 book titles) to a high of 6,958 (in a library holding 1,650,440 book volumes). Many libraries reported extensive audiovisual holdings in many media, including multiple microformats, sound recordings, videorecordings, films, filmstrips, maps and charts, overhead transparencies, slides, and art reproductions.

Library incomes ranged from $147,000 to $9,558,000, with six libraries with less than $500,000 and twenty-six reporting more than $1,000,000.

MEDIUM-SIZED PUBLIC LIBRARIES

Sixty municipalities with populations between 50,000 and 150,000 were surveyed for the study, including cities in thirty-four states. Some of these smaller cities also were part of the greater metropolitan areas of larger cities, e.g., Livermore, California (San Francisco), East Hartford, Connecticut (Hartford), Dearborn Heights, Michigan (Detroit), Brentwood, New York (New York City), Niagara Falls, New York (Buffalo), and East Providence, Rhode Island (Providence).

Some of the public libraries were in towns where well-known colleges or universities also were located, e.g., Boulder, Colorado; Hattiesburg, Mississippi; and Bryn Mawr, Pennsylvania.

Twenty-two of the public libraries called themselves county or regional libraries, or the equivalent, and two more had names indicating that they served more than one community or municipal entity. Two called themselves library systems. One was known as a library association.

Book holdings of the sixty public libraries ranged from

34,017 volumes to 382,545. Periodical subscriptions ranged from none (reported by nine libraries) to 1,241 (in a library holding 121,654 books). Most of the libraries reported having audiovisual holdings, with only twelve failing to list any, but many of them did not indicate the number of items in each format, or gave totals without specifying the distribution of formats.

Circulation statistics varied from a low of 98,000 items a year (for a library with a collection of 28,393 book volumes, 100 periodical subscriptions, and a variety of AV items) to a high of 1,118,096 per year (for a library with a collection of 220,000 book volumes, 1,100 periodical subscriptions, and no reported AV holdings).

Library incomes for the public libraries ranged from $166,000 to $3,047,000, with six libraries having less than $500,000 and nineteen libraries reporting more than $1,000,000.

THE RESPONDENTS

Telephone calls were placed to the chosen libraries to determine who had overall responsibility for the technical service unit to which the survey questionnaire should be sent. In some instances, the call merely confirmed the names of the persons listed in the *American Library Directory* entry for the library, or their replacements. If no technical service unit head was given in the entry, the appropriate librarians and their titles were identified.

Twenty-nine of the sixty academic library respondents were titled "head" of the unit or an equivalent, i.e., "chairperson" or "director" of the unit, "chief" technical services librarian, or, simply, technical services librarian. Among the thirty-one academic librarians contacted who did not have "technical services" in their titles, fifteen were general administrators with titles such as "director" (also, associate or assistant director), "dean," and "head librarian"; eight more were heads of cataloging units. The remaining eight librarians had a variety of titles, some of which could be interpreted as having primary duties of a different nature: documents librarians, serials librarians, director of acquisitions, head of materials services, head of monographs, coordinator of library services, etc. Two of the technical service titles had "data processing" and "automated services" added to them, indicating that library computing was a subunit reporting to the administrator of the technical service unit.

Of the sixty public librarians, thirty-three had "technical services" (or, in one instance, just "technical") in their titles. "Head" of the unit was still the most frequent specification, but, in the public sector, alternatives to that designation included "coordinator" and "supervisor" as well as technical services librarian, technical services processor, and technical processor; none was called director or chairperson of the unit. Among the twenty-six public librarians contacted who did not have "technical services" in their titles, twenty-two were directors, assistant directors, or librarians, and none were called dean, head or chief librarian. Only two had "catalog-" in their titles: one cataloger and one head of cataloging. The remaining two librarians were called "head of processing" and "head of the support services division."

The Responses

NUMBER AND TYPE OF RESPONSES

Sixty-one librarians filled out and returned the eight-page questionnaire. Thirty-one chose to remain anonymous. Of those who identified themselves, seventeen worked in academic libraries and thirteen worked in public libraries. In all, responses were received from twenty-seven academic libraries, twenty-eight public libraries, and six libraries whose type could not be determined.

THE TECHNICAL SERVICE UNIT

Fifty of the libraries referred to the unit handling the functions of acquisition, cataloging, etc. as "technical services." If this group is any indication of general practice, it seems technical services is the overwhelming favorite over all alternatives, including support services (one), processing services/ center (two), bibliographic services (none), or the cataloging department (two). Five librarians said there was no overall technical services unit in their libraries, and two of them noted further that each component group reported directly to one or more administrators who oversaw some, but not all, of the services covered by the questionnaire. One person did not respond to the question.

Six separate subdivisions within the umbrella unit were identified on the questionnaire: acquisition/order (called acquisitions below); serials control (called serials); cataloging and classification (called cataloging); processing/binding (called processing); circulation/inventory control (called circulation); and collection management. All but eight of the libraries subdivided the umbrella unit. Three respondents noted that the functions were divided, but activities in different subunits were performed by the same staff because they did not have enough staff members to go around.

When technical services had two subdivisions (nine libraries), they tended to consist of an acquisition unit, sometimes including serials, and a cataloging unit, sometimes including processing and binding. Less often, the two-division technical service unit consisted of monographic and serials subunits. Two libraries included circulation control as one of two subunits while one library included interlibrary loan as a subunit with cataloging.

Three subunits was the most common organizational structure, occurring in fifteen libraries. The functions most frequently included in the tripartite substructure were acquisitions, cataloging, and processing, although three libraries subdivided their technical services unit into acquisitions, serials, and cataloging. Only one of the fifteen libraries in this group included any other function—in this case circulation—as a discrete subunit along with cataloging and processing.

Thirteen libraries had four subunits in technical services. All but one of these libraries included acquisitions, cataloging, and processing as three of the four subunits. The unique organizational structure was acquisitions, cataloging, serials, and circulation. As for the other twelve libraries, the fourth subunit grouped with acquisitions, cataloging, and processing was either serials or collection management in all but one, where government documents was named as the fourth technical services subunit.

When five subunits were identified under the technical services umbrella (at eight libraries), all but one included acquisitions, cataloging, and processing among them. Other subunits included serials, circulation, collection management, and/or computing for all but one library, which named interlibrary loan as the fifth subunit. The unique structure did not include cataloging, but named acquisitions, serials, processing, circulation, and collection management as its five subunits.

Six or more technical services subunits were identified by six libraries, all of whom named acquisitions, serials, cataloging, and processing as four of the subunits. Three of the six also named circulation and three named collection management. Of the respondents who identified the other separate subunits, two named gifts and exchanges; two named assorted library-wide administrative activities, including accounting, mail room, telephone, etc.; one named services such as card production and catalog maintenance that might be subsumed under cataloging elsewhere; and one named government documents.

Clearly, the one central function most frequently identified as a technical service subunit is cataloging, followed by acquisitions and processing services, then serials, circulation, and collection management. Computing services (also called systems or database management), government documents, and interlibrary loan occur more than once as parts of umbrella technical services units.

Staffing of the technical services unit in the sixty-one public and academic libraries responding to the questionnaire ranged from a low of .5 to a high of 153.5 full-time equivalent staff positions, averaging thirteen staff per unit. Two academic and three public libraries had fewer than three staff members, while two academic and two public libraries had more than twenty-five. Six technical service units had no professional librarians, but excluding these libraries, the group averaged 2.7 professionals per unit. Twenty-four of the libraries had just one professional librarian in the unit.

Dividing the library types showed the public libraries tended toward smaller units with fewer professional librarians than did the academic libraries. The public libraries averaged twelve staff per unit, 1.4 of them professional librarians, while the academic libraries averaged nearly sixteen staff members per unit, 3.4 of them professionals.

The position of the technical services unit within the library's general administrative structure varied, too. One question dealt with the person to whom the unit head reported, offering the following possibilities: unit head is the chief library administrator; unit head reports to the chief administrator; unit head reports to an associate or assistant administrator. If none of these applied, the respondent was asked to fill in the appropriate organizational status. Overall, the unit head was the chief library administrator in two libraries; in forty-six, the unit head reported to the chief administrator; and in eight libraries, the unit head reported to an associate or assistant. Four responses named alternatives, including supervisors, coordinators, or branch librarians, all seeming to be lower in the hierarchy than associate/assistant directors or their equivalents. One respondent did not reply.

Dividing the libraries by type, in one public library, the unit head was the chief library administrator; in seventeen, the unit head reported to the chief administrator; and in six, the unit head reported to an associate or assistant. In one academic library, the unit head was the chief library administrator; in twenty-four, the unit head reported to the chief administrator; and in two, the unit head reported to an associate or assistant. (These total fifty-one responses. Four respondents did not answer these questions and six did not identify their library type.)

From these replies, one could conclude that, for this group of libraries at least, the public and academic library technical service units were at a similar level in their library's organizational hierarchy: the second level (i.e., a majority of each type reported directly to the chief library administrator).

This is not an unexpected finding, since libraries are typically divided into public and technical services units and in medium-sized libraries the heads of these units might be expected to report to the chief library administrator. Given the relative sizes of the units and the numbers of professionals in them, one might have predicted that the academic library units would be slightly higher in the organizational structure. This is reflected in the data, which showed the proportion of technical service unit heads reporting directly to chiefs was larger for academic libraries, while the proportion of unit heads reporting to associates or assistants was larger for public libraries. There was no statistical significance in the difference, however.

In the next chapter, the use of computers in technical services is explored.

—2—

Computing in Technical Services

A Review of Pre-Computer Systems

"Manual systems" is an umbrella term for all the systems used to accomplish technical services functions before the era of computer-based data processing. Many of these systems were not entirely manual; they employed machinery of some sort, e.g., typewriters to prepare order records or catalog cards, printers and duplicating machines to reproduce catalog cards, automatic stampers to imprint a patron's borrowing number on a book card, or cameras to take a microphotograph of the book card and borrower's card, used with microreaders to decipher the records for overdue materials. Tauber particularly specified photographic services (other than those related to circulation services) as a technical function, and listed a number of media production services which the technical services department might be expected to provide. These services included photostating statistical tables, advising doctoral students in the preparation of illustrative material for dissertations, and making overhead transparencies, filmstrips, and slides for faculty members as well as microfilming materials and maintaining microform readers.[1]

In the 1980s, media production services have been spun off from technical services. Microphotographic services often are called the "microfilm" (or microform) unit, "reprographics," or some variation on that theme, and it is not unusual to find them paired outside the technical services unit with government documents, serials, or preservation units. Other types of media production, such as making transparencies, preparing photographs, slides, etc., frequently are not done within the library at all, but in a central media production facility, sometimes linked with printing or duplicating services. It is more likely one will find in-house media production facilities in academic libraries than in public libraries, which tend to rely on commercial services for such production.

The distinguishing feature of the manual systems used in all of the managerial aspects of technical services, however, was that they resulted in the production of paper records that had to be filed in paper files that grew to very large size, even in medium-sized libraries. The maintenance of those files depended upon the labor of human filers. Some manual systems relied on human labor entirely, even for the preparation of their paper records, requiring that the order slips or catalog cards be generated by typing or hand-writing them (still common for circulation slips).

The personnel employed in technical service departments using manual systems, even in medium-sized libraries, represented a very large chunk of the library's budget. The cost of all this labor mounted as libraries expanded and wages and inflation increased in the post-World War II era. Academic libraries grew along with college and university programs that accommodated returning soldiers whose tuition was paid by the federal government. Public libraries grew, too, as the children of this generation of college-educated men and women—known as the "baby boom" generation—moved through the various stages of their elementary and secondary schooling, then went on themselves to college and post-baccalaureate programs in increasing numbers.

All technical service operations grew as the production of library materials expanded to "information explosion" proportions, and infusions of federal funding into libraries fueled a futile race to keep up with it by acquiring as much material as possible. Once purchased, these materials had to be processed, cataloged, circulated, preserved, etc., creating a crisis in technical services operations that reached major proportions.

Two problems emerged in library technical service departments in the 1960s: (1) slow processing and the concomitant build-up of huge backlogs of unprocessed or incompletely processed materials (e.g., major university filing backlogs were alleged to be measured in years, not days or months, of staffhours); and (2) sharply rising unit costs as wages and inflation both rose throughout the decade. Response to these problems included renewed efforts to share the burden of buying and processing materials, but by decade's end, librarians looked to computers to provide solutions.

Computerized Bibliographic Systems

Systems employing computers, generically termed automated systems, were introduced into a small number of pioneering libraries toward the latter part of the 1960s. The first computer-based systems employed large, expensive mainframe computers, and accomplished a great many tasks in offline, batch mode processing. These systems might more appropriately be termed computer-assisted, since they usually were not directly online with library operations as they occurred and processing of transactions was done separately from the execution of the transactions themselves. Instead of taking weeks, months, or longer, updating could be accomplished overnight or within a few days; but this speedier turnaround time still fell short of instantaneously updated files each time a transaction was executed (e.g., completing an order, cataloging a book, checking a book in or out, or passing a date due without the return of a borrowed item). Instantaneous updating could only take place if operations were online and tasks were processed as the data were input, with all files and indexes being adjusted automatically.

Few medium-sized libraries might have hoped, then or since, to own their own mainframe computers, but some, as well as larger institutions, could take advantage of campus or municipal computers purchased primarily for administrative tasks such as billing, payroll, registration, etc. They could also have access to the "free" expertise of programmers employed by the parent body who developed appropriate software for the system. Naturally, no service is truly free, and elaborate systems of chargebacks began developing in universities and elsewhere to allocate appropriate levels of cost to libraries in return for the services being rendered by computer centers and their staffs.

At the end of the 1960s and beginning of the 1970s, two separate developments occurred to spur the introduction of computers into library technical services. The establishment of the Ohio College Library Center (OCLC, now known as the Online Computer Library Center) by forty-eight Ohio college and university library directors and their appointment of Frederick Kilgour to direct the creation of a cataloging data processing center was the first. The second was the application of Digital Electronics smaller-sized minicomputers to library circulation control by Bela Havatny, who founded the firm currently known as CLSI.

In 1970, CLSI began marketing its minicomputer-based system programmed for circulation control services based on a Digital Electronics Corporation PDP-11 series central processing unit (CPU) that cost approximately $20,000. The entire package of hardware, software, documentation, system support, training, and ongoing development purchased by a library might add up to a total of $150,000 to $200,000, excluding the cost of encoding the library's patron and holdings data into digital form and inputting it into the computer. "Hardware" meant much more than the CPU, since all the terminals, light pens or scanners, printers, modems, and associated cabling that might be needed were included, too, as well as the storage media—disk drives, disks, magnetic tapes, or other devices—on which the local database was expected to reside. Although CLSI was among the earliest suppliers of computerized bibliographic systems, it was quickly joined by competitors, in increasing numbers with each passing year. That same year saw the inauguration of

OCLC's card production services, albeit in off-line batch processing mode.

The Growth of Library Computing

A little more than a decade later in 1980, a survey by Boss and McQueen of automated circulation control systems listed fifteen different vendors, of which CLSI was still the largest in terms of the numbers of installed systems or annual sales.[2] This number varied continually as vendors entered and left the marketplace, sometimes going out of business and occasionally being bought up by other companies. In addition, there were vendors who concentrated on providing other functional services, such as serials control, acquisitions, and cataloging. A few vendors provided more than one functional service, and touted their systems as being "integrated."

By 1980, three other national networks known best by their acronyms had joined OCLC as major originators and processors of bibliographic data: UTLAS, RLIN, and WLN. UTLAS was an acronym for University of Toronto Libraries Automated System, a data processing group within the Canadian university that began developing a bibliographic system for its own use, but broadened its mission to serve other libraries in Toronto and elsewhere throughout Canada. This network is now a profit-making corporate subsidiary of the Thomson Companies known as Utlas International, and it serves libraries in Canada, the United States, Australia, Europe, and elsewhere. RLIN stands for Research Libraries Information Network, the data processing unit of the Research Libraries Group formed originally by the New York Public Library and Columbia, Harvard, and Yale universities. RLIN remains a nonprofit entity and continues to serve a small constituency of research institutions from its headquarters near Stanford University in northern California. WLN, first the Washington Library Network and later the Western Library Network, began as an arm of the Washington State Library providing libraries in the state and, later, in contiguous states with cataloging data processing. WLN is no longer part of the state government and became a private, nonprofit corporation.

Also by 1980, the Library of Congress and the National Library of Canada were distributing their computerized catalog records via magnetic tape to libraries directly, if they subscribed to the MARC (MAchine Readable Cataloging) Distribution Service, or indirectly, through inclusion of their MARC tapes in all four major network databases.

Nearly a decade later, toward the end of the 1980s, the library world experienced a proliferation of turnkey[3] and quasi-turnkey vendors.[4] Annual surveys of automation vendors in the 1980s[5] listed more than twice as many companies in the library automation marketplace as in the previous decade, and the companies had to be divided according to the types of systems they offered:

• systems that provided solely an individual function vs. systems that performed several functions in one integrated system;
• variations in the completeness of the turnkey package, including software only, software plus some other components, or complete systems; and,
• differences in the type of computer involved, i.e., minicomputers, microcomputers, or workstations.

Two factors probably contributed to this proliferation: (1) the emergence of affordable, powerful microcomputers and other equipment associated with microcomputers, such as CD-ROM disks;[6] and (2) considerable experience with the programming necessary for dealing with bibliographic data. Bibliographic records were thought to be nearly impossible to program because of their length, variation, and complexity. But software designers dealing with non-library language-based elements succeeded in developing database management software with widespread application in business and industry that immediately proved easily adaptable to bibliographic systems.

In the latter part of the decade, as the numbers of players and their activities increased remarkably, annual surveys gave way to constant monitoring of the automation marketplace by many journals, especially the popular library press.[7] At the same time, the Library of Congress, OCLC, WLN, and some of the state and regional networks began devoting large proportions of their resources to computing, creating and distributing a variety of computer-based bibliographic products of all kinds to the library community that could be employed with standard makes and models of mini- and microcomputers. Although most of the new products supported cataloging, they were not exclusively concerned with cataloging and featured serials control, collection development, acquisitions and fund accounting, and reference tools.

Causes for the remarkable increase in automation activity are understandable. From the library manager's perspective, computers were the best thing since sliced bread:

1. Once in place, computer-based systems could handle a considerably larger workload efficiently with the same number or fewer staff members
2. The computer-based system furnished more and better services to library patrons with its high-tech, flashy-looking white, green, amber, or multicolored flickering screens
3. The costs of computing, especially storage and processing power, were declining constantly.

From the technical service librarian's point of view, once they were in place, computerized systems provided:

1. More opportunities for access to a much larger pool of bibliographic information through networking and thus, greater potential for service;
2. Greater variety in the alternatives available for storing, organizing, retrieving, and displaying bibliographic data in local systems;
3. Better methods of controlling workloads and balancing the larger workloads of the information explosion and fewer available staff hours for handling it with the computer's capacity for efficient data processing; and, finally,
4. A tremendous vitality created by the growth of a national database made up of the many local, regional, national, and international systems.

Issues in Library Automation

Among the important issues in library automation that have emerged since its beginning in the 1960s are the following:

1. The relative value of system packages that include all the components necessary for quick implementation—turnkey systems—versus the purchase of various components from different vendors, with the library assuming the responsibility for combining them into a working system;
2. The relative value of purchasing different systems to perform the various functions of technical services and, then, linking them to one another, versus purchasing one system that integrates all of them;
3. The quality of user interfaces, i.e., the ease or difficulty with which members of the library's staff or the lay public could use the computer system as well as other types of human-machine relations issues such as the health risks of doing computer work, physical plant and furnishing requirements for computing, etc.;
4. The degree of comprehensiveness of the system, primarily the question of whether and how to put all the library's already existing non-computerized bibliographic data into the system;
5. The extent to which a library would implement all possible features of the automated systems it purchased or leased, especially the capacities for larger numbers of access points, access from outside the library, links with other internal and external systems, electronic delivery of documents, with or without sound and graphic enhancements, and more; and,
6. The organizational responses to changes in workflow and internal connections among departments resulting from the automation of bibliographic services, which made all computerized information available to any staff member with a terminal.

One additional issue that emerged in the latter 1980s was the development of library collections of computer-related materials and the degree of inhouse computing services that might be provided to patrons by libraries.

A Closer Look at the Issues

TURNKEY SYSTEMS VERSUS PURCHASE OF COMPONENTS

The advantages of the component approach was that the library could select standard hardware which was usually less costly and sometimes more efficient than proprietary hardware (i.e., hardware produced by the vendor/proprietor that could only be supplied by the vendor/proprietor) and could be maintained more effectively by a local dealer. Also, librarians could opt for desired variations in such aspects as the methods used to identify materials (e.g., eye-readable labels versus barcoded labels) and enter data into the system (via scanners, magnetic tape, input by hand, etc.). Generally, with a "do-it-yourself" system, the library retained greater control over system configuration, features, implementation, ongoing operations, and maintenance.

At the same time, the do-it-yourself, build-your-own computer system approach required that the librarians know a great deal more about what needed doing and how best to do it—knowledge that very few librarians possessed in those pioneering days. Libraries were likely to be faced with an immediate need to hire staff competent in computing but lacking sufficient understanding of library functions, or, conversely, to have staff competent in the functions of library operations, but lacking sufficient understanding of computing to make important and costly decisions. The two groups of people seemed poles apart in their approaches to problems as well as to solutions, and complaints, each about the other, appeared frequently in the library literature.

The alternative was to purchase a turnkey package including, at the least, the hardware and software needed to provide some technical service function, e.g., ordering, cataloging, or circulation control. Other package components usually included the following:

- maintenance of the hardware and software
- general system support
- initial installation of the equipment and basic software
- vendor-led staff training or staff training materials for the library to implement
- subsequent improvements in the software
- special consideration in the purchase of improved hardware, and,
- general consulting—advice about what the library needed in the way of data processing and how to obtain it.

Turnkey vendors did not routinely build their own computers, although some did and still do; they were more likely to buy computer components from various manufacturers and combine them with minor alterations so they might honestly claim the hardware was unavailable from other sources. Some vendors merely combined standard hardware components without alteration, but in doing so, they saved the librarian-purchaser from having to select the appropriate parts and put them together into a working system. When standard hardware components were used for a turnkey system, the price charged to the library-customer might reflect actual costs to the vendor with a surcharge for handling and overhead, or all of those charges plus an added profit factor.

The software, on the other hand, was likely to be the vendor's own product, either completely self-programmed or a customized variation of a standard software product. Some of the vendors of the 1980s grew out of self-programmed systems developed for the pioneering libraries of earlier decades, e.g., the NOTIS system, which originated at Northwestern University; the VTLS system, which originated at Virginia Polytechnic Institute and State University; and the DYNIX system, which originated at Brigham Young University. Librarians' natural inclinations to share a good thing with colleagues plus the opportunity to recover part of the enormously high cost of initial development probably contributed to this phenomenon. In these instances and others, however, units handling such systems eventually became private, nonprofit corporations separate from their parent institutions or profit-making companies.

All of the turnkey components other than hardware and software might be supplied at varying levels without charge, with separate charges, or not at all, depending on the vendor and the turnkey system involved. As computing became less complicated and more user oriented, the need for training and installation services diminished, while maintenance and system support for hardware might be contracted out to third parties. Generally, system support for software had to be handled by the vendor, since it was a proprietary product. One turnkey component that was rarely part of early packages, but now is frequently a highly-advertised feature, is conversion of a library's existing paper files into a computerized database.

SINGLE-FUNCTION SYSTEMS VERSUS INTEGRATED SYSTEMS

There are two ways to computerize the technical service department, based on two fundamentally different approaches: develop a different system for each function, or develop one system with different software modules for each function. In the early days of library computing, system developers managed to address only one of the technical services functions at a time, although they promised and tried to develop multiple functions from the beginning. Libraries, too, tended to be interested primarily in computerizing one function at first, then expanding to other functions with the same system or some other system. Very often, the constraints of budgets and/or inadequate facilities and staff limited the amount of computerization an individual library could undertake, while the capabilities of computer hardware and the state of software development limited what could be done with available equipment, staff, and funding.

In general, public libraries seemed most concerned about computerizing acquisitions and circulation control, while academic libraries seemed most concerned about computerizing acquisitions, cataloging, and serials control, although such was not always the case. Vendors tried hard to write programs that could use the same database for different functions, but success was elusive in the 1970s and early

1980s. Different developers produced systems that focused on different functions, and almost inevitably, none of them was compatible. If a library wanted to computerize its circulation system and ordering functions, it might have to purchase three different systems using three different computers from three different vendors—one for the circulation function and one each for acquiring monographs and serials. In the 1970s and early 1980s, incompatibility with other vended systems was a positive marketing factor (i.e., the vendor was certain only another proprietary module or system could be added to whatever was being sold); but in the late 1980s, this changed to some degree, with some vendors claiming to be compatible with all systems conforming to the library-wide MARC standard,[8] and others listing the names of systems to which they could easily be linked.

People spoke about the possibility of linking incompatible systems. One of the first such links or interfaces was built to enable a bibliographic record from the OCLC network database to be automatically transferred to a local CLSI circulation control system. Since that successful interface, others have been developed between disparate systems, based for the most part on the Library of Congress' MARC communications format for bibliographic data. The MARC format was adopted very early by library computer networks and subsequently by computer vendors serving the library market. In the decade of the 1980s, other standards that address networking issues, such as the International Standards Organization's Open Systems Interconnection Reference Model (OSI) were developed and promoted on national and international levels. Although the capability exists to connect disparate systems using OSI and other standards, it is not implemented routinely and even those systems that purport to support it have done so only incompletely. Nevertheless, networking technology is improving rapidly, and the expectation is that the 1990s will be the decade of networking.

An integrated system, i.e., one using a single local database for multiple functions, is an ideal toward which developers strive, since it is the most efficient and economical way of using the database and requires the fewest linkages. However, although several vendors offer more than one function and many claim to have an entire range of technical service modules, none of them can demonstrate in practice that their system can do absolutely everything that librarians do in technical service departments. Some systems are capable of performing some, but not all, of the tasks in several functions, e.g., creating order slips, but not maintaining fund data, or creating a holdings file for serial issues, but not automatically flagging the librarian when an issue is overdue, or creating bibliographic records and public access displays, but not linking authority control records, or creating inventory records (i.e., item level or holdings information), patron records, and borrowing records, but not accommodating hourly loans common in academic libraries' reserve rooms.

Librarians now are offered a great many options for systems in all sizes and price ranges that do excellent jobs with a single technical service function or related set of functions as well as for integrated systems that perform basic tasks in more than one technical service function. Choosing among the available alternatives, never an easy decision, has become more difficult and complicated than ever. And, since progress in computing continues at a dizzying rate, the full-service integrated system able to do all the bibliographic data processing described in the balance of this book might appear soon.

USER FRIENDLY INTERFACES

Operation of computers before the 1980s in many settings, but especially in libraries, required extensive costly and time consuming training. The person who sat down at the computer terminal, with its glowing screen and keyboard, had to be a reasonably competent typist, since a misplaced space or an erroneous punctuation mark might confound the information request. He or she also had to know exactly which commands, in what sequence, would cause the system to perform the desired work and produce the desired results. Library systems were called "unfriendly" or "user-hostile," because methods by which someone using the system communicated their requests, called the "user interface," were complicated and difficult to learn. Computing was largely restricted to library staff, who were taught to do whatever was necessary.

When computing services for public use began to be designed, user-hostile interfaces were clearly unacceptable. Efforts to design the kinds of screens that made system operation easy and obvious were not immediately rewarding and early public access computers were hampered by long instruction sheets or manuals, or self-training sessions requiring a major investment of the user's time and energy.

One of the early user-friendly catalog interfaces designed by CLSI employed a screen with touch sensitive pads with which users could select a desired request from a series of menus. First, the person pinpointed the type of desired request, then worked through a broad range of potential answers, narrowing the number of options until the desired record was found. (Similar computers are found in large supermarkets to help customers locate particular items.) This might have been fine for a beginner with time to spare, but it quickly became frustrating for experienced searchers who knew what they were seeking or did not have the time to conduct a leisurely search. Experiments such as this one demonstrated that different kinds of interfaces might be needed for beginners and knowledgeable searchers.

Librarians and library-computer vendors persisted and endeavored to improve their initial efforts. By the end of the 1980s, attention by computer experts, librarians purchasing computer systems, and companies producing and selling the systems, began to achieve a measure of success in creating easy-to-use screens. These did not frustrate beginners by being too difficult or veteran users by requiring long sequences of simple steps that could not be overridden. Multicolored displays, text highlighting, thoughtful data placement, understandable text labelling, and other formatting devices were employed to improve the way data was displayed. Some vendors went so far as to make their screens look like catalog cards, hole and all, in order to make the computer-based catalog as "friendly" and comfortable as the old card file. Function keys that replaced complicated or lengthy command sequences with the touch of one key were used, and the function keys were labelled with understandable words such as "STOP" or "SEARCH" instead of codes such as F1 or F2, as well as being color coded or highlighted in other ways.

No doubt easier to use, more convenient interfaces between people and computers will be designed in the future, but the improvement in technical service screen displays during the decade of the 1980s was nothing short of spectacular. Computer systems employing different hardware and software have differing capabilities for ease of use. Interfaces employed in technical service systems have become an important feature, since public access catalogs are frequently part of these systems. These developments are similar to what happened with public service computer systems: user interfaces became important as soon as decisions were made to market them directly to those persons seeking information—the end users—instead of to professional database searchers whose job was to mediate between the system and the information seeker.

OTHER HUMAN-MACHINE INTERACTIONS

Virtually an entire industry has sprung up to address the problems of humans using computers, from the design and marketing of specially-proportioned furnishings—tables, chairs, terminal turntables, screen filters, etc.—to medical research on the potential health risks of exposure to rays from video display terminals, constant use of backlighted screens (as opposed to use of paper-based printed materials) and other computer-related phenomena. Common sense tells us that furnishings designed with computers in mind will prove to be more convenient and appropriate than tables, chairs, etc., designed for other purposes. While a library might be inclined to save money in its initial automation project by making do with existing furniture, it sometimes proves wiser to buy furnishings properly proportioned for use. Otherwise, comfortably positioning the paraphernalia computer users require—printers, paper, disks, manuals, telephones, etc.—will be very difficult.

Library buildings, especially older ones, designed without enough electrical outlets, telephone jacks, and space for cabling as well as areas sufficiently large to house computer tables, storage facilities, etc., found themselves in need of repairs and redesign to accommodate all of these environmental necessities. Some libraries wished to house computers in secure areas and, in all instances, the physical environment needed to be kept free of magnetic fields, static electricity, and potential hazards associated with temperature and humidity extremes.

A deeper issue is related to the general working conditions of computer operators, i.e., staff users as opposed to members of the general public. Although research has not fully confirmed the existence of health problems associated with computer use, anyone might develop backaches, eye fatigue, and related ailments from sitting in one position looking at a computer screen for many hours at a time. While it might sound innocuous for a person to be assigned to do copy cataloging forty hours a week (after all, assignment to a single type of task for many hours is typical of many jobs), it has proved disadvantageous in practice. Instead, many libraries have adopted personnel policies limiting the number of hours staff users may sit at their terminals without a break, and have deliberately varied staff responsibilities to avoid grievances or allay fears that the institution is negligent or uncaring.

CONVERSION OF EXISTING DATA

As mentioned above, implementation of a computer system in a library benefits greatly from the conversion of existing bibliographic data into computer-readable form and its integration with data for materials acquired after the system is put in place. In the early 1970s, librarians were told they could build their databases by entering the data for items acquired before the computer when those items were handled for other purposes, e.g., when they were borrowed, when they were replaced by newer editions, when they were sent to the bindery, etc. This process was called conversion "on the fly." It was haphazard and often resulted in enormous data entry backlogs that sat in back rooms while the materials themselves were borrowed, sent to binders or to other libraries for interlibrary loans without the owning library maintaining any control over them. Even for libraries with small collections, this rapidly became a problem.

Conversion of bibliographic data for pre-computer holdings, or "retrospective conversion," "recon," and/or "retrocon," as it came to be known, elicited great attention as libraries with large collections began to computerize. It was time consuming and costly to enter these collections into computers on a title-by-title basis, yet the computer system was far less effective without the data. If a library belonged to a bibliographic network, it might obtain archived records of its cataloging in computer-readable form and enter that data into its computer automatically. However, many of the errors and anomalous practices permitted in cataloging departments over the years showed up to complicate the data transfer. Furthermore, before 1980, quite a few local library computer systems were not programmed to accept the MARC-formatted network data, there were no scanners to read typewritten or printed text directly into computers, and few conversion services existed which could do the job at reasonable prices.

The decision to build the library's database by converting data in card catalogs and other manual files was a serious commitment for any library, even a relatively small one. For example, if a library had 100,000 titles and data for each of them took two minutes to enter into a computer, the whole collection required 200,000 minutes or more than 3,333 hours to convert. At $5.00 per hour for a computer operator, without the added costs of employee benefits and without the time employees must reasonably spend gearing up for work, at breaks, and preparing to leave, the price of complete conversion was nearly $17,000. During the 1980s, some libraries took advantage of federal grants to libraries or job training grants in order to convert their pre-computer holdings to machine-readable form. Some libraries decided that retrospective conversion in their institutions could only be done partially, while others decided not to think about it until after initial computer implementation.

It is not unusual for a library to have several catalogs in different formats, with some of the holdings entered into each one. This not only destroys the catalog's ability to perform its functions effectively, but makes it more costly to maintain and use. Some library administrators believe they must wait until they succeed in obtaining grants or special allocations to convert the balance of their data or until a newer, less costly method can be devised to do the job.

REALIZING SYSTEM POTENTIAL

Five elements contribute to success in realizing the computer system's full potential: building a complete database; acquiring a system of sufficient size and power; providing adequate training to all staff and non-staff users; organizing operations and procedures to utilize the computer system to fullest advantage; and tailoring policies to exploit the capabilities afforded by the computer system.

One of the problems of failing to complete retrospective conversion is that it prevents the library from realizing the computer system's full potential. The savings in staff time and the benefits of new services and information only apply to the holdings for which bibliographic data are in the database. If none of the previous holdings are entered, implementation of the computer system will be the least effective and most costly, since manual operations have to continue at the same level as before computer implementation, but the computer system also has to be maintained. Elimination of the manual system is a step that must be taken, eventually, before the full potential of the computer system is reached.

Computer systems need to be of sufficient size and power to support the desired number of terminals, store all the necessary data, and provide all desired functions. Purchase of a smaller system with fewer features might fit a library's budget, but it could fail to do the job for which it was intended.

Adequate user training—both staff users and members of the public—is another factor that impacts the effectiveness of a computer system. Even systems with friendly user interfaces require training for some functions. Without the requisite knowledge, users cannot enjoy the full benefits of the computer system. Having too few terminals sometimes results in limiting the number of people who are able to receive training and use the system. Allowing trainees too little time to practice what they learn also contributes to errors and misuse of the system. While gaining familiarity and dexterity with the system is most critical in the implementation period, there will always be new users who need time to learn the system.

Traditionally, bibliographic instruction (or library instruction) has been the library's educational function for lay users. The literature of bibliographic instruction reflects the important place computer-based systems occupy now, with much attention being paid to explanatory handouts, reference cards (refcards), handbooks, and manuals designed to introduce patrons to online public access catalogs, computer-based indexing and abstracting systems, etc. Sometimes there is insufficient communication between the bibliographic instructors, typically reference librarians, and the technical services staff responsible for maintaining the online public access catalog. Such gaps in communication are unfortunate for all concerned, especially the patrons, and when they are discovered, should not be permitted to continue. Technical and public service librarians need to work together toward common goals for the benefit of library patrons.

ORGANIZATIONAL CHANGES IN RESPONSE TO COMPUTERIZATION

Most important of all in getting everything one can from a computer system, however, is the realization that pre-computer organization, operations, and procedures will change in response to system capabilities. Preparation for changes in workflow, careful monitoring of procedures, and experimentation with new ones are difficult tasks. Even more difficult is the realization that staff job descriptions will change as some jobs are done automatically by the computer system while other jobs are created. Morale among employees whose jobs are in transition can sink to dangerously low levels if efforts are not made to clarify and ensure job security and to consider human reactions to the changes in the library. Along with organizational changes, policies that were based on the limited information and control possible with manually-maintained files need to change in response to the availability of more information and the greater control possible with the computer system.

According to Neal,[9] once a library's computing operations are mature and full bibliographic information (i.e., not only catalog records, but acquisition and circulation information, etc.) is available throughout the institution, the traditional division between public and technical services becomes useless, or worse, a barrier to optimal use of resources. In libraries at the University of Wisconsin, Penn State University, Yale University, the University of Illinois, and elsewhere, reorganizations have focused on combining responsibilities that require professional judgments to be made and creating dual-role assignments (i.e., in public and technical services) for librarians that encompass only one of these types of tasks. Thus, a librarian might have a job description that includes selecting materials, answering questions at the reference desk, and cataloging materials for which bibliographic information is unavailable from network databases for a limited subject or language area in which the person has special expertise, e.g., Kampuchean history or German literature. Managerial duties such as training, planning new services, etc., might be added to these tasks.

Reports in the library literature of such reorganizations are found in larger numbers each year, as are justifications for undertaking them despite the upheavals they cause during implementation. Ruschoff mentions administrative reorganization of technical services units as one of the chief trends in the field revealed by her analysis of the literature of cataloging and classification in 1989.[10]

LIBRARY COMPUTER COLLECTIONS AND IN-HOUSE COMPUTING SERVICES

Simultaneously with the changes occurring in processing library materials and furnishing library services due to computerization, some libraries decided to build collections of computer materials and provide computer laboratories for public use. The acquisition of computer materials requires decisions about technical processing, and librarians have chosen to handle them in different ways: in some libraries software is treated exactly like all other materials, while in others, the computer laboratory and its software are treated as special collections with special processing systems.

Obvious issues with which managers must deal are the design and implementation of the physical environment for the computer laboratory and the development of the collections of hard- and software. Other less obvious but equally important issues are the kinds of policies the library establishes for use of the materials. Since ownership of computer software is not always part of the purchase—many software packages are leased and their contracts contain specific obligations on the part of the leasing library—it may be necessary to limit the use of software to the laboratory instead of circulating it like other library materials. And since copying expensive copyrighted software is so easy, the library has to take responsibility for educating its patrons about legal and ethical practices.

Almost all libraries instituting public use computers have experienced heavy demand for them, which has spurred growth of facilities. As a result, what might have started as a single computer, perhaps matched with a very small special collection, suddenly becomes a computer laboratory combined with a major flow of new materials through the technical services unit. Handling computer software requires new types of expertise for selecting, ordering, cataloging and classifying, and processing, the material. Different approaches to the problem have been taken by different libraries, but sometimes the most computer-knowledgeable people are found among technical services staff. The role of technical services may, thus, be heavily involved in computing facilities and materials. Another approach is to separate computing from the rest of library services. In such instances, technical services staff will experience little change in their work.

Microcomputers and Workstations

As the eighties progressed and microcomputers—also known as personal computers—became widely available for just a few hundred dollars (for the smaller ones) or a few thousand dollars (for standard-sized IBM PCs and Apple II or Macintosh computers), almost every library could afford them. Without doubt, the 1980s became the microcomputer decade. Software for microcomputers proliferated, sold by established vendors who also offered systems based on larger computers, and new vendors entering the market for the first time with homegrown software products. Even the smallest libraries entered the computing marketplace, buying simple programs to print catalog cards or produce overdue notices.

Microcomputers grew smaller, more powerful, and less costly throughout the decade until, in 1990, some of the smallest machines costing less than $5,000 were more powerful and handled more data than the original CLSI Digital minicomputers of the 1970s costing at least four times as much. The ease with which additional data storage could be purchased and connected to a basic microcomputer system and the development of computer operating systems with flexible, user-friendly interfaces revolutionized the potential for library computing.

At the same time, some microcomputers were being augmented by newer technologies and developed into workstations—systems in which the microcomputer was just one part of a much larger combination of equipment and software. Intner describes workstations as falling in the price range of $10,000 to $60,000, and being "a more powerful machine that is connected, usually through a network, to other machines of similar or greater power."[11] In addition to its powerful microcomputer system, a workstation might include CD-

ROM disk drives, telecommunications links, network links with other microcomputers, interactive video capabilities, and more. Intner says, "There are multiuser workstations, graphics workstations, diskless workstations, and combinations of the three."[12]

Thus, the choice of computers and computing software is rapidly becoming the determining factor in a library's data processing systems (bibliographic data operations). Whether a medium-sized library considers itself large enough for a now more-powerful minicomputer or is satisfied with minimal microcomputing capabilities might mean the difference between having online public access catalogs with linked authority files, integrated acquisitions and circulation modules, and gateways to electronic mail systems and nationally-distributed databases, and having an offline electronic card file, in which limited bibliographic information is stored on a CD-ROM disk and updated a few times a year. The former is state-of-the-art; the latter is one-tenth the price, but it might not be as up-to-date or as complete as a well-maintained card catalog, even though it is searched via a video display terminal. The saving grace of the latter, however, is the enormously flexible searching afforded by even the simplest and least costly CD-ROM-based public access catalog that far outstrips any card file in speed and sophistication.

Data Processing for Technical Services

All data processing functions of technical services have been computerized. Computer systems have been programmed to write orders, communicate them electronically to a publisher's or a vendor's receiving computers, manage finances, report claims, check in new materials (both monographic and serial), support all cataloging operations including providing authority files and shelflists, produce labels, provide public access to catalog information, maintain patron files, and keep track of all borrowing records, including fines and fees. Although the technology is available and the software exists, no one system "does it all" successfully and is in use, *yet.* Nevertheless, even as these words are being written, the development of bigger, better, more complete, and less costly technical service computer systems continues, and it is only a matter of time until libraries are offered an ideal computer system for technical services data processing.

Computing in the Surveyed Libraries

One academic librarian, discussing her general reactions to the survey instrument, said, "You didn't ask enough questions about computers and data processing. Everything in tech services today is computers, computers, computers." In general, the survey responses bear out that claim. Only three public and two academic libraries reported lacking any computer systems at all in their technical services operations. One of the three public librarians commented, after writing "None" in the space for the responses to questions about computing, "Preparing to go online soon."

Even among libraries that already were using computer systems, some new systems or changes to old systems were underway. Comments indicated that seven libraries were somewhere in the process of seeking, acquiring, or implementing a new or different computer system.

Cataloging was the technical services function most frequently computerized in the surveyed libraries. Nineteen public and twenty-one academic libraries reported having computer-based cataloging systems. Both circulation and the acquisition of monographic books were computerized in eighteen of the public libraries responding, but only eight reported having computerized serials control and still fewer said they had computerized collection management support. In contrast, fifteen academic libraries reported having computerized systems for monographic acquisitions, fourteen had computer-based serials control systems, and fourteen had computerized circulation control systems. Four academic librarians reported using computer systems for collection management.

One distinguishing feature of the responses from academic

and public libraries was that, although many of the libraries used more than one computer system, academic libraries almost always reported using more than one. It was not unusual for the academic library responses to indicate use of a different computer system for each function that was automated. The majority of the multiple systems described were the use of two systems for cataloging: a bibliographic utility (e.g., OCLC, WLN) for the cataloging process and a local system for the catalog display. In addition, the bibliographic utility also was used for interlibrary loans. The local system sometimes also was used for purposes other than cataloging.

Conclusion

Many would say that library data processing began with cataloging, i.e., with OCLC and Utlas, the two oldest bibliographic utilities, and was extended later from cataloging to other public and technical service functions and services based on bibliographic data. It is not unusual for the library's technical services department to be responsible also for local data processing. Arguing for broad training in automation for catalogers, Iowa State University's library director, Nancy L. Eaton, writes, "automated library systems [are bringing] cataloging and indexing systems within the same operational framework . . . As databases are added to the library's online system, the distinctions between the library's catalog and other information databases become less obvious."[13]

Acquisitions and Collection Management

Acquisitions and collection management are two aspects of the building of library collections. As used here, "acquisitions" refers to the processes and systems of ordering and obtaining library materials, while "collection management" includes decision-making about collection goals and objectives, allocating the materials budget, what to buy to meet collection goals, selection of individual titles or groups of titles, and evaluation of the collections.

Unfortunately, the term "collection management" does not have one clear and precise definition. It is used here because it appears to be a popular umbrella term for acquisitions and related activities, some or all of which are performed in the technical services unit. Terms used as synonyms for collection management include "collection development," "resources management," "collection building," and "collection maintenance," although each of these designations also may have different meanings.

Librarians appear to define collection management as the processes of selecting and acquiring library materials, but individual libraries define it as they choose. Collection management activities may be considered wholly or partly within the realm of technical services, or wholly or partly within the realm of public services, depending on an individual library's emphasis on the acquisition or selection responsibilities. A survey of sixty Association of Research Libraries members published in 1974 showed that these institutions were divided on the placement of collection management units in their organizations, with approximately 60 percent putting them in bibliography departments, i.e., public services, or in acquisitions departments, i.e., technical services. The report goes on to say, "The ongoing responsibility for materials selection tends to be . . . diffuse. . . . Acquisitions librarians are reported as having some selection responsibility in nearly every institution, although a minor one in most."[1]

Tauber, et al., who devoted five chapters of *Technical Services in Libraries* to acquisitions and collection management, identified the following activities as part of the acquisition process: preliminary activities; checking and searching; bibliographical preparation; placement of orders; receiving, billing, and distribution; and claiming and cancelling.[2] Whether and how these activities are performed in the medium-sized libraries sampled will be discussed below. Tauber discussed the acquisition of monographic books and serials together, as well as government documents, dissertations, and a variety of nonbook materials, assuming that all of these materials would be handled by the same department. One of the changes that has occurred since the 1950s is the rise of separate serials units, sometimes within the acquisitions unit, sometimes elsewhere under the technical services umbrella, and sometimes under the reference or public services umbrella, as well as separate units for nonbook media materials and services, and government documents.

Two developments seem to have allied serials with reference units: the use of indexes, kept in the reference unit, to access articles in serial publications, especially periodicals; and the designation of serials as non-circulating, placing them with other non-circulating reference materials. While individual libraries divide materials in different ways, printed serials are commonly housed separately from books, either with or near reference collections, and responsibility for acquiring and managing them may be separate, too. If the lion's share of microform collections are serials, microforms may be located with or near other non-microform serial holdings, and responsibility may be combined with that for other serials. Similarly, government documents may be found under the managerial umbrella of the reference unit whether they circulate or not, because special tools, special knowledge of government agencies, and special ordering procedures are required to acquire them. (Some libraries even charge reference librarians with cataloging government documents and maintaining the catalog.) Non-circulating nonbook materials, especially maps, also may be a subset of the reference collection and responsibility for acquiring them assigned to the reference department.

Nonbook materials, other than maps and microforms, rarely are part of reference collections. More typically, nonbook media materials, including films and videos, printed and recorded music, visual materials, laboratory materials, models and other objects, and computer-based materials are combined into one or more special collections, and responsibility for acquisition and collection management as well as cataloging of these materials often is assigned to that special unit.

Pre-Order Collection Management Activities

SETTING COLLECTION GOALS AND OBJECTIVES

Collections are created specifically with purposes in mind, purposes that, in an ideal world, are aimed directly at the people who will use them. In medium-sized public libraries, the people include the residents, taxpayers, and non-resident workers, students, and visitors in the political jurisdictions to which the libraries cater. People from surrounding jurisdictions also may be accommodated by contract or by mutual agreement with the libraries in those jurisdictions. In medium-sized academic libraries, the people include the students, faculty, administrators, alumni, and visitors at their colleges and universities, and such non-affiliated persons as the institutions decide they will serve.

Each library's parent body, whether it is a municipality or

an academic institution, has a mission statement, usually found in its charter and often repeated on important documents such as its annual reports. Each library also has a basic mission statement, found either in its charter or in a part of the parent body's charter. Ideally, it is to the basic missions of the parent body and library that collection managers will go to start a search for appropriate collection objectives, because all library activities must be in harmony with those statements if they are to be successful.

Next, one might expect that the search for objectives will be based on careful analysis of data describing current and future client populations, matched with librarians' expert assessments of their information needs and interests. Gathering such data is not easy, but it is a critical element in maintaining rapport between the library and its clients, and it has been the focus of much attention in the field. The *Public Library Mission Statement* and other library standards reflect this concern with relevant collections, and methods of determining what relevance is for individual libraries.[3] Strategies for compiling statistical data and methods of using them to achieve library goals and objectives are the subject of several books from the American Library Association.[4]

Demographic statistics must be sorted to reveal the relative numbers of persons who can be served by the library in various age groups, occupations, educational levels, academic disciplines, etc. Community or campus activities can be studied to see what they are and who participates in them, what kinds of organizations are present and how they operate, and who belongs to them and why. The information needs and interests of the public are determined by talking to people in all the relevant groups, by asking questions and listening to answers, and by making a concerted effort to find out what issues and concerns are important to each group and each person contacted. There is no such thing as having too much knowledge of one's clients. Most important of all, librarians must be concerned not only with people who are regular users of the library, but also with those who are not, especially those who do not use it at all, although they qualify for service.

All the statistical data and relevant knowledge about the community or campus and information interests and needs then must be sifted and interpreted, preferably through a group process but at least through a sustained effort, to give fair consideration to each potential interest and need before objectives are formulated. Collection goals and objectives are best when they result from a translation of the public's needs and interests into target strengths in subjects, languages, media, audience-levels, etc. Collection goals also must harmonize with the library's basic mission, and the objectives should express in measurable terms what the library will try to achieve in a particular collecting cycle.

ALLOCATING MATERIALS BUDGETS

Competition for limited funds is to be expected, and can be resolved by the assignment and balancing of priorities that reflect the persons and information needs or interests the library chooses to serve. The objectives and priorities are the agenda for collecting, and this agenda logically should drive the allocation of funds among the library's divisions.

The process just described is an ideal scenario for formulating collection goals and objectives, from which materials allocations are derived. Some libraries do not have written collection goals and objectives, but operate on the basis of intuitive judgments, formulae that make incremental changes to existing allocation patterns, or by allowing designated selectors to do what they think best without attempting to coordinate their efforts into a library-wide set of objectives. Interest in written collection development policies with explicitly identified, measurable goals and objectives based on research into user needs has intensified throughout the decade of the 1980s for several reasons. First, the real value of library budgets has been shrinking steadily as prices rise and information production increases; second, administrators want to spend their dollars as wisely as possible on materials everyone agrees are the most important; third, funding authorities are beginning to demand evidence showing that monies have been well spent; fourth, the process of establishing goals and objectives gives members of the library's staff and community opportunities to express and clarify their needs; and fifth, written goals and objectives protect the library from those who claim to be unfairly treated or ignored.

Since Elizabeth Futas published her first compilation of library acquisition policies,[5] interest in written policies has grown and demand for more existing models engendered a number of additional publications.[6]

EVALUATING COLLECTIONS

Once an agenda for the collection has been established, librarians naturally ask the question: How does the existing collection meet these objectives? What are the strengths and where are the weaknesses in the collection? The answers lie in a careful evaluation of library holdings performed from two perspectives: quantitative and qualitative.

The quantitative evaluation examines observable facts about holdings in a particular subject, language, or other designated area, such as the number of items held and the media in which they are manifested, how old they are on average and the distribution and pattern of publication dates, and in what condition they appear to be. A single quantitative evaluation gives a profile of the library's collection at a particular point in time, and can answer questions such as "How current are the science materials?" and "Are holdings in history adequate to satisfy accreditation standards?" Comparison of the current profile with previous statistics can answer questions such as "Are French literature holdings growing to match larger numbers of French majors?" or "Is the condition of U.S. history materials better now than it was five years ago?" Comparison of the current profile with similarly drawn profiles of peer libraries, i.e., libraries whose sizes, populations served, and general missions are very similar to those of one's own library, can answer questions such as "Do we have as much material in computer science as our peers?" and "Are our holdings in consumer information more or less current than those of Community X?"

Objective measures of quantity, age, media patterns, and condition are important, but they do not, by themselves, reveal the quality of the materials. However, certain gross judgments about quality can be drawn from them based on general criteria. One such judgment is simply that more material is better than less.[7] Another is that newer holdings are better than older ones, which may be true for some disciplines such as science and engineering, but is definitely false for others, such as history and literature. A third very obvious judgment is that holdings in good condition are better than holdings in poor condition.

Observations for performing qualitative evaluations differ from those made for quantitative evaluations. They measure the library's holdings against standards of quality. Among the most commonly used standards of collection quality are lists of important works, such as authoritative bibliographies, guides to the literature of a field, catalogs of libraries accepted as excellent, etc. When this kind of evaluation is performed, librarians must do more than make careful observations; they must decide, in advance, what will constitute excellent, good, fair, and poor showings of their collection against the standard. The list-checking observation can tell only that n percent of the titles in the list are held by the library. It does not determine whether n percent is a good showing or a bad one, or whether the titles included in the n percent held are the most important titles. Also, the list checking method does not reveal whether other titles held by the library but not on the list might be as good or better than some titles on the list that were not held. Comparison of one's holdings to authoritative lists also begs the question, "Is it appropriate that my library have all the works on the list?" Futas and Vidor make this point in their comparison of the holdings of Emory University's business school library with those of Harvard University's Baker Library.[8]

Another measure used for qualitative evaluation of the collection is the number and pattern of interlibrary loan requests for materials not held locally. These observations are more revealing over time than they are at one point in time, e.g., it is a clearer indication that a collection strength exists for a field if interlibrary loans decrease for that field than if they increase, if they are small with respect to the total number of interlibrary loans, and/or if the library is a net lender in that field. A similar observation can be made by reference librarians about the ability of local holdings to satisfy patron requests.

A different kind of quality judgment may be made about collections by examining patterns of use. This is easier said than done, according to Katz, who says, "When evaluation is linked to the shape of the collection, one enters the sensitive area of how much attention the librarian should pay to user demand, particularly for popular materials. If the librarian is on the side of quality, the public may be less than enthusiastic. Conversely, one may adopt the Baltimore County Public Library's approach by evaluating collections in terms of popularity, and not only buying titles that are much in demand, but purchasing multiple copies. Here it seems possibly at the expense of others."[9] McGrath suggests that we lack paradigms for describing collection use, and suggests several possibilities.[10] But an earlier study of collection use at the University of Pittsburgh demonstrated a pattern known as the "80/20 rule," i.e., that 80 percent of material use is satisfied by 20 percent of the titles in the collection.[11] The Pittsburgh study seemed to confirm the suspicions of funding bodies that libraries buy a great deal of material they don't really need and could do without. Simple counts of material circulations or in-house use are helpful as one of several measures performed in a qualitative evaluation, but probably should not be trusted as the sole measure of quality.

The lack of standard measures for collection evaluation that would enable all libraries to make the same kinds of observations and apply the same kinds of criteria to the results has been a problem for a long time. Whenever one library compared its statistics with those of another library, there was no way to know whether enough similarities in the measures existed to enable valid comparisons to be made. One cannot always tell if a "volume" in one institution is counted the same way it is in another, since some libraries include periodical volumes, sound recording albums, etc., in the volume count, while others count only monographic books, or include individual pamphlets and maps. The definition of fields of study also can differ widely among institutions, e.g., at Emory University, economics is a part of the business school, while at Northwestern University, it is part of the arts and sciences. Similarly, the definition and placement of computer science departments may emphasize engineering, mathematics, communications, business, or information science.

The Research Libraries Group has made great progress in establishing standard measures for dividing collections for evaluation purposes, in describing intended collecting scope and coverage, and in measuring the condition of materials. The tool they have developed, the *RLG Conspectus*, is maintained as an online file in the RLIN network, so the information is available instantly for its members.[12] The *Conspectus* structure and software has been adapted and used by other groups to support planning for cooperative collection development.[13]

In the final analysis, subjective interpretations of all of these objective measures taken together must be made, and conclusions drawn about the strengths and weaknesses of collections. As more objective evidence is gathered to support particular conclusions, librarians are able to have greater confidence in them, and in the goals and objectives based on them.

SELECTION AND APPROVAL

Most acquisition units begin with the assumption that titles have been selected for purchase by staff in another unit, but this is not always true in small and medium-sized libraries. The unit most likely to be responsible for selecting titles for purchase is the public service or reference unit, primarily because it is made up of subject experts or bibliographers who also perform reader's advisory services. In a good many libraries, however, all professional librarians are responsible for selecting titles in one or more disciplines; and in some, the acquisition librarian is also the bibliographer, spending part of his or her time in each role.

In some libraries, the director reserves the right to coordinate selection activities and must approve all selections before they can be sent to the order department. Although requiring the director's personal approval of all selections may seem extreme, it is not necessarily a dictatorial stance, since he or she, as CEO, is both the final arbiter of budget allocations and ultimately responsible for all complaints about materials. Depending on the library's parent body, the CEO, the librarians, the policies, and the communities involved, placing selection power in the hands of one person might be a reasonable procedure. Some CEOs review selections and give pro forma approval, reserving the right to veto only those titles they believe to be totally out of scope, too costly, or otherwise inappropriate for the library. Some review selections only for certain fields, media, or audiences, or only items costing more than a designated amount.

At the other extreme is the CEO who takes no part in selection activities, but delegates all responsibility for them to others. Ultimate responsibility for selection might be assigned to one collection management or collection development officer or to a group of selectors, usually the bibliographers, or perhaps, all professionally-educated librarians regardless of their other duties.

For most libraries, selection is a shared task and responsibility for approval also is shared, at least to some extent. Many different models exist and are employed. Often, heads of subject-, medium-, or audience-oriented departments and branch libraries select and approve titles for their departments and branches, although they, too, may choose to parcel out the job to one or several members of their staffs. There may be a selection committee with a relatively stable membership or a rotating membership. In academic settings, selection may be partly or completely within the hands of teaching faculty. Librarians might select titles and faculty approve them; faculty might select titles and librarians approve them; or both librarians and faculty might select titles, leaving the coordination of all selections and final approval to a designated staff member, a faculty-library committee, or the library's CEO. Libraries whose selection is driven entirely by the requests of teaching faculty sometimes find that their collections become seriously skewed and incoherent when faculty select solely those items relating to their highly specialized research interests. Futas and Vidor found that faculty can contribute positively to the selection process, and it was not clear that librarians always did a better job of selecting titles.[14]

Both academic and public libraries frequently have policies of purchasing titles specifically requested by patrons without requiring that the usual procedures be followed, but they reserve the right to turn down a request if it does not seem reasonable.

Whatever methods are employed to select materials and whoever is charged with responsibility for giving final approval to the selections, once the process is completed and approval is obtained, pre-order searching usually is the next task.

PRE-ORDER TASKS

Before a title is ordered, someone in the library needs to ascertain that the item does, indeed, exist, and that it is not already part of the active holdings of the library (unless it is an intentional duplication or replacement). Assuming that these tasks have not been performed by the selectors in the course of the selection process, pre-order searching and bibliographic verification are the first steps in the order process. Logically, it is most efficient to check the library's catalogs first and, if the item is not found, then to verify that the data is correct and sufficiently complete for ordering.

Librarians rarely are assigned to do pre-order searching, although they are responsible for training the people who do it. The search of the catalog and verification of the bibliographic data generally are done by paraprofessionals, clerks, or even pages. Pre-order searching sounds more complicated in theory than it turns out to be in practice, since the selector can be expected to supply titles, authors or editors, and, probably, other important data such as editions, publishers or distributors, years of publication, series titles, etc. Verification also tends to be fairly mechanical, since selections usually are made from review journals, publisher's notices, or other sources whose stock in trade is providing trustworthy data for purchases.

Search problems can and do occur if selectors submit patron requests without knowing or checking on their accuracy, cost, or relevance to the collections, and library policies should insure that they are verified and approved by a knowledgeable librarian at some point before they are ordered. If orders are placed for patron requests without any verification at all, the library might find it has acquired and is responsible for some extraordinarily costly or inappropriate items it might not have chosen to purchase otherwise.

Acquisitions: Ordering and Obtaining Library Materials

Responsibility for ordering and obtaining library materials is almost always a technical service activity. The steps that Tauber outlined for the acquisition process still must be done, and they form a logical sequence that is convenient to follow: placing orders; receiving, billing, distributing materials; and claiming and cancelling.

ORDERING AND RECEIVING

The first step in placing an order is deciding where to place it, i.e., to which vendor of library materials to send it. For some titles, there is no choice involved because they can only be obtained from their publishers, or by joining an organization for which the publication is a right of membership. But for many titles, there are several alternative sources, including their publishers, general distributors of library materials, specialized distributors, and bookstores, some of whom have wholesale operations designed to serve libraries. Medium-sized libraries that buy trade books might be well served by purchasing them from a single general distributor, provided that they negotiate contracts specifying agreeable discounts and that the service they receive meets or exceeds their expectations. Libraries of any size that buy specialized materials including foreign language materials, nonbook materials, materials from small presses, or other sources outside the mainstream publishing channels, will probably need other sources for these items.

Before computing, orders were placed by preparing individual order slips for each title being purchased or by combining titles to a multiple-title order sheet. With manual files, the advantage of individual slips was that carbon copies could be filed by author, title, or another desired element in an order file that could be searched for any one item. Computing has altered order processes to some degree, although order slips or multiple-title order sheets may still play a part in the computer-based process. Now, however, the slips may be generated by the computer to be sent to the vendor from whom the purchase is being made. Perhaps the most important difference in computer-based ordering for the library is that a file of carbon copies no longer need to be maintained. It is replaced by a computer database that can be accessed at multiple terminals and searched by a variety of access points. Computerizing orders saves the high cost of labor-intensive filing, does a more accurate job of recording and filing, and provides for broader dissemination and more sophisticated retrieval of the information.

Order slips and order sheets are not the only means by which items can be ordered, either now or in the past. Before computing, orders could be placed by telephone, or items could be purchased directly by librarians, without the preparation of order records at all. The latter option is rarely exercised by libraries, since it is not a systematic method, but telephone orders for some items, particularly rush order materials, is not uncommon. Computing has added a new variation on the telephone order, in which libraries use their telephone or computer communications software to access the vendor's computer, then punch in the Standard Address Numbers (SANs) for each unit of the library desiring to order, followed by ten-digit International Standard Book Numbers (ISBNs) for each title ordered for the unit. Deliveries can be made to a central location or to each location for which there is a different SAN.

Problems occur with telephone ordering when ISBNs are not available for desired titles and/or when these orders are not automatically recorded by the library in their local database or non-automated order file. If a telephoned order is not in the vendor's stock and must be back ordered for the library, it may take several weeks before this information is reported in writing, and several more days before it is disseminated to the relevant units. In the meanwhile, there is no record of the transaction, and other selectors might ask for the same items, resulting in unwanted duplicate orders. And, of course, it always is a problem if the numbers are entered incorrectly and the wrong item is ordered.

Another way of obtaining materials is through the use of approval plans. Approval plans are a method of buying quantities of material in a field by allowing the plan's vendor to supply all the titles that match a set of specified criteria, e.g., being assigned a particular Library of Congress or Dewey Decimal classification number. Approval plans can be useful to medium-sized libraries even though they were designed primarily for large libraries. The critical factor is the library's ability to identify sufficiently precise specifications for enough materials to make it worthwhile for the vendor to serve them in this manner.

The initial impetus for approval plans and other mass gathering schemes came from a desire to obtain materials more quickly and cheaply. The former was accomplished by having materials shipped without the usual time devoted to reading reviews, selecting individual titles, approving them, searching and verifying them, and placing orders for them. The latter was achieved because the cost of selection was borne by the vendor, not the library; all the library had to do was specify categories of materials, all of which were wanted. During the 1960s and early 1970s, when library budgets were augmented by federal monies and colleges and universities were at the height of postwar expansions begun in the 1950s, a strong feeling arose that it was better to gather and discard a few undesirable items than to miss one desirable item that would be difficult to obtain later.

Public librarian Emerson Greenaway launched the first gathering plan by agreeing to take copies of all titles brought out by certain publishing houses. These selected houses were known for their high quality publications, most of which were likely to be wanted. The publishers agreed to send the books to the library when they sent out pre-publication review copies, giving the librarians lead time to decide what they would select and order in multiple copies for the city's many branches and central library collections. Greenaway believed it was worth taking a few unwanted titles in order to get the remaining titles before publication.

Approval plans differ from Greenaway's plan, which was called a "blanket order" plan, in that libraries deal with distributors, not publishers, who permit a small proportion of materials to be returned. In other words, the materials are sent to the library "on approval," and there is a brief time in which the library can decide whether or not they will keep them. In practice, if too many titles are returned to the vendor, the library will be asked to revise the criteria by which selections are made or be dropped from the plan.

Receiving ordered materials when they arrive and recording their receipt usually are the next tasks after placing orders. Materials are checked to ascertain that the items received were those that were ordered, and to indicate on the order record, whether in paper or digital form, that the item was received. It now is the library's job to keep track of the items' physical location as well as to indicate to the accounting officer that the bills for them should be paid.

FINANCIAL MANAGEMENT

Billing, according to Tauber's description, includes what is now termed "fund accounting," i.e., the process of tracking how much money is encumbered and spent in each separate budget allocation or fund category as well as keeping a running tally of the total amount being spent. Allocations may be divided by subject, language, department, audience, medium, branch, or by their combinations (e.g., a branch library's children's department picture book collection, or a geography department's map collection). Within each unit's total allocation, monies might come from more than one source, compounding the record keeping. Periodic financial reporting to responsible librarians may be part of the acquisitions officer's responsibilities.

In some libraries, the acquisitions officer completes all the financial transactions, not just authorizing payment, but issuing checks to pay vendors. In addition, financial records require updating to show that encumbered funds were paid out as well as to give the new set of fund balances.

Computerizing fund accounting makes an enormous difference for the acquisitions librarian because the labor-intensive recording of fund balances, encumbrances, and expenditures can be done automatically by the computer when materials are received and the data entered. Not every computerized acquisitions system can provide automatic updating of individual funds, balances, etc., however, and librarians cannot assume these capabilities are always provided. The two processes of order and receipt and financial tracking are related, but they involve different types of computational tasks and many kinds of specification. Librarians need to recognize that programming all the necessary tasks with a broad range of specifications and linkages is a complicated (and therefore costly) development effort, and not one that computer system vendors should be chided for finding difficult to provide in system packages of reasonable cost.

OTHER METHODS OF ACQUIRING WANTED MATERIALS

Purchase is not the only way to obtain wanted materials, although it is the way most are acquired. Some wanted materials are received as gifts and some are available from other institutions or organizations in exchange for items desired by those institutions or organizations. Activities performed in connection with gifts and exchanges of materials may be assigned to acquisitions librarians or they may be handled by someone else, usually the library director, the development officer, or the rare books or special collections officer.

Many libraries accept gifts of materials and some actively seek them, but most are careful to have policies governing the process. Policies will cover issues such as what will be accepted, how the gifts will be acknowledged, whether librarians will estimate the value of gift materials for donors, whether the library will accept conditions imposed by donors, how the materials will be handled, and who has the right to decide. Usually, libraries will not accept gifts given on condition that the library handle them in a particular way, e.g., to keep the donated collection together, to house it in a special room, etc., although they frequently place bookplates in gift items to identify their donors. Librarians also shy away from assigning monetary values to gifts that donors will use for tax deductions, since such evaluations might carry legal culpability if they are erroneous. Some libraries refuse to accept certain types of gift materials such as paperbacks, magazines, and older nonbook media in formats that are no longer popular. Most will accept anything, however, as long as the library retains the right to throw away, sell, donate, or otherwise dispose of items not wanted for the collections.

Libraries of any size that wish to acquire rare or out-of-print materials, or primary research materials such as letters, memoranda, personal records, photographs, artifacts, etc., may hope to obtain these kinds of materials through gifts from generous donors. Success in obtaining valuable materials from donors requires patience and knowledge on the part of librarians as well as tact, perseverance, and luck. Libraries cannot rely on gifts to fill their basic needs, but they may provide unusual resources, particularly for historical and special collections.

Gifts may consist of more than books and other library materials; they may be in the form of money, equipment, furnishings, land, buildings, stocks and bonds, or other valuable items. As library budgets have tightened, gifts have become more attractive as an alternative source of support for the library, and they should not be overlooked or ignored.

Exchanges in which one library sends available publications to another in return for wanted items depends largely on continuing agreement between the partners. Traditionally, this meant keeping up an ongoing correspondence. Success depends on having publications that a partner wants, wanting the titles the partner has to exchange, and negotiating mutually agreeable transactions.

The exchange process is time-consuming and labor-intensive, since it involves research, writing, and negotiation. Libraries that wish to dispose of duplicate copies, in-house or intrainstitutional publications, or hard copies of titles being converted to micro- or digital formats stand the best chance of having materials to exchange. Finding exchange partners is another issue, however, and there is no one channel through which one can locate them. Traditionally, libraries in academic institutions or other organizations outside the United States tended to be interested in exchanging their publications for those of U.S. libraries.

As educational, scientific, and trade publishers have developed global distribution networks, however, the exchange market has dwindled, and librarians' interests in continuing their efforts to cultivate and maintain exchanges also has diminished. Sometimes libraries cannot give away their unwanted duplicates, etc., and organizations set up to facilitate exchanges, such as the United States Book Exchange (USBE), have found it difficult to survive.

Post-Order Collection Management Activities

EVALUATING COLLECTIONS, AGAIN

Since collection evaluations are a major effort, they rarely are done more than once during a collecting cycle, but it is useful for collection managers to re-examine parts of the collection toward the end of a cycle to see whether they seem to be reaching the goals and objectives set at the beginning of the cycle. It also is useful to track whether ordered titles were received for each department or branch, to analyze those that were not received, and to examine how effectively individual library suppliers performed. Such evaluations might become an important factor in negotiating new contracts with these vendors.

It may not be possible to do a second evaluation before the end of the cycle, especially if the cycle is short, e.g., a semester or less than a year. If, however, the cycle is longer than one year, e.g., a five-year plan, it could be disastrous to wait until it is over before assessing the ongoing effectiveness of acquisitions. At the rate titles go out of print, it might not be easy to go back and fill a gap that occurred because an important group of ordered titles did not arrive.

When the next full evaluation is done, it is with new goals and objectives in mind, and the successes and failures of the previous cycle will become the basis for the current cycle.

WEEDING, STORAGE, AND REPLACEMENT

Chronologically, reviewing individual titles for retention, storage, replacement, or discard follows their acquisition and use. Philosophically, however, these activities are linked more closely with the initial selection of titles for inclusion in the collection. Psychologically, it is difficult to generate as much enthusiasm for reviewing holdings as for selecting new materials, since it goes against the collector's grain to throw anything away. But review is a necessary and important activity in managing collections so they do not grow beyond the capacity of the library and its users. Medium-sized libraries in particular may experience space problems as new materials are added and very little of the older material is removed. When a library's policies require that nothing ever be discarded, materials deemed marginal to current needs or in such poor condition they cannot be used may be placed in less accessible areas or in off-site storage facilities. Removal to less accessible storage also is an option for materials that librarians believe are not needed immediately, but may have value in the future and, therefore, should not be discarded.

Two attributes of less accessible storage areas are important to consider: suitability of the physical surroundings for storing library materials and the length of time required for retrieval. Before basements, back rooms, storerooms, top floors, or other little-used or out-of-the-way places are brought into service as storage areas for weeded materials, physical conditions should be investigated and steps taken to control heat, humidity, infestation, etc., and to provide shelving, lighting, air circulation, and routine cleaning services that will promote extended life for the materials. Otherwise, stored materials could deteriorate so rapidly that they might as well have been discarded. If the library cannot provide the necessary storage environment, it might be advantageous to rent or purchase space in a remote storage facility that does, even though it is off-site. The length of time required to retrieve an item from less accessible storage needs to be determined as well as the staff who will be responsible for retrieval and return of the materials to the storage area. Some libraries have succeeded in providing requested materials to patrons within a few minutes with on-demand retrieval from on-site storage areas. Others need up to two or three working days to obtain a requested item from a remote facility.

Factors that will affect library decisions about on-site versus off-site storage are the total cost of a storage site (i.e., the cost, spread over a reasonable period of time, of preparing and maintaining a suitable in-house site and the cost of renting or buying and maintaining a comparable remote site), the number of items that will need retrieval, the distance to the storage site, the staff hours available, travel options to a remote site, and the kind of service the library wishes to provide.

Less accessible storage is not free of cost, and the largest of the costs is likely to be the initial preparation of a library-owned storage area or the ongoing cost of a rental site. Other costs include moving the materials from the main stacks to storage, maintenance of the storage area, and staff time needed to retrieve and replace stored materials when they are requested and returned.

Moving some older materials to less accessible storage may stave off space problems for some period of time, but no finite physical plant can absorb increases in collections forever. Medium-sized libraries will want to think ahead and calculate how much material can be housed in active collection areas before shelving space is filled, and then plan how they will house more materials long before they reach that point. Often it is a space crisis that motivates weeding projects, even though weeding should be as continuous an activity as selection.

Some of the questions asked when an item already in the collection is reviewed are the same as those asked when an item is selected for acquisition: Does this item meet library goals, objectives, and policies? Is this item in a subject area of interest to patrons? Does this item contain information believed to be accurate, well-written or produced, representative of its kind, or otherwise important to library users? New questions also are appropriate, e.g., does the condition of the item warrant retention? Has the item been superseded by a new edition or by newer titles with more up-to-date coverage, broader scope, or more thorough treatments? Is the medium appropriate to user needs, or is the title now available in new or different media? These do not exhaust the possibilities, but are representative of the kinds of questions weeders will ask in reviewing materials for removal from the active collection.

When it is clear that an item should be removed, librarians turn to the next decision: whether to keep the item somewhere else, to discard it and replace it with a new copy or a new title, or just to dispose of it. There are several options for disposal, including selling the material in a library book sale, donating it to another library, or quietly putting it into a dumpster. Although it may be appropriate and reasonable for a library to destroy unwanted materials, the action can be misunderstood by some who think valuable resources are being thrown away. Thus, disposal of materials is a delicate and unpleasant task that probably should be done as discretely as possible.

Acquisition and Collection Management
Units in Surveyed Libraries

Separate acquisitions units were reported by thirty-eight institutions. Most of these were staffed by at least one part-

or full-time librarian plus three or more non-professionals including paraprofessionals, clerical staff, assistants, and/or pages. Public library units were much smaller than their academic counterparts, with public libraries reporting having at least three support staff far less often than academic libraries. Among the academic libraries, most said they had at least five support staff members working in the acquisitions unit.

Virtually all the respondents said they maintained order files and nearly as many had separate standing order files as well, the latter sometimes combined with serials order files. Fewer libraries (about half or less of the public libraries and more than half of the academic libraries) also had vendor, invoice, and fund files. Public libraries reported having vendor files more frequently than the other types of files, while academic libraries had invoice files most frequently. Fund files were maintained least often by these libraries.

Not all the responding libraries reported conducting preorder searches, with sixteen reporting doing none. Fewer academic than public libraries did pre-order searching, with thirteen of the academic libraries reporting they did none. When academic libraries did do pre-order searching, unit heads were as likely to do the searches as clerical or support staff. In contrast, only three public libraries reported doing no pre-order searches; in those that did such searches, clerical or support staff performed them three times more often than unit heads. The files most likely to be searched before orders were placed were the order and standing order files and the public catalog, but many fewer libraries searched public catalogs than order files.

Financial reports were prepared by nearly all the librarians responding to the survey, and statistical reports were a close second. About half the public libraries also furnished acquisition lists for staff or patron use, but only about one-third of the academic libraries did so.

Seven public libraries and thirteen academic libraries had separate serials units. All but five were headed by librarians. Academic library serials units were quite large, with most reporting having six or more additional support staff members. Public library serials units were quite small, with only three having as many as five support staff in addition to the unit head.

Lists of serial subscriptions, holdings, and serials statistical reports were prepared often, either by the serials unit or the combined acquisitions/serials unit, but more academic libraries produced all three than did the public libraries. Holdings lists were more likely to be prepared in public libraries than in academic libraries.

Asked to describe the unique features of their acquisition systems, some librarians focused mainly on their computer systems, writing comments such as:

"dBase III inhouse database includes fields for all bibliographic data, encumbered amount, actual cost, order date, received date, etc., claims, and status fields"

"Almost all verification is done on OCLC. Orders are printed directly off of OCLC onto a multipart purchase order form. A sophisticated online fund management system is used to track encumbrance/receipt of books and generate vouchers for payment of all materials."

"We have all our standing orders on OCLC's SC350. It is wonderful for claiming."

"Relies heavily on electronic ordering systems."

"Unit utilizes in-house microcomputer-based system for acquisitions work. Records are downloaded from OCLC and form basis of on-order file and fund accounting."

"All files maintained on Commodore microcomputer using a database management program."

Other respondents used the space to explain their staffing arrangements or division of responsibilities in greater detail, e.g.:

"All staff members have duties in other Tech. Services areas. The paraprofessional spends about 85% of her time on acquisitions work. The other staff spend less than ½ time . . ."

"Book selection is done by librarians and ordering process is done by clericals."

"We are a branch campus of a major university. We prepare our orders and maintain our own books, but actual placing of orders with vendors, processing of invoices and official budget control is handled for all campuses at our main campus location."

And last, but not least, one librarian summed it all up by stating simply, "It works."

Conclusion

The acquisitions function is central to technical services, and includes the procedures that bring materials into the library. Important tasks in the acquisitions unit include administering bibliographic and financial data and interacting with publishers, vendors, and other librarians. It is not unusual to find these tasks combined with complex decision making for overall collection building, including the formulation of collecting goals and objectives; allocation of funds; selection of materials for purchase, discard, and storage; and the regular evaluation of existing collections. Together, acquisitions and collection management activities provide the first of a library's obligations to its public, to gather collections of materials.

Suggestions for Additional Reading

Acquisition Policies in ARL Libraries. Washington: Association of Research Libraries, 1974.

Bonn, George S. "Evaluation of the Collection." *Library Trends* 22 (Jan. 1974):265–97.

Collection Development Policies. Washington: Association of Research Libraries, 1977. (SPEC Kit #38).

Curley, Arthur and Dorothy Broderick. *Building Library Collections*, 6th ed. Metuchen, NJ: Scarecrow Press, 1985.

Evans, G. Edward. *Developing Library and Information Center Collections*, 2d ed. Littleton, CO: Libraries Unlimited, 1987.

Futas, Elizabeth and Sheila S. Intner, eds. "Collection Evaluation." *Library Trends* 33 (Winter 1985):237–43.

Johnson, Peggy. "Dollars and Sense," bimonthly column in *Technicalities*, beginning with vol. 9, 1989.

Katz, Bill. *Collection Development: The Selection of Materials for Libraries*. New York: Holt, Rinehart, 1980.

———. *Magazine Selection: How to Build a Community-Oriented Collection*. New York: Bowker, 1971.

Kohl, David F. *Acquisitions, Collection Development, and Collection Use: A Handbook for Library Management*. Santa Barbara, CA: ABC-Clio, 1985.

Lancaster, F. Wilfrid. *If You Want to Evaluate Your Library . . .* Urbana, IL: University of Illinois Graduate School of Library and Information Science, 1988.

Lockett, Barbara, et al. *Guide to the Evaluation of Library Collections*. Chicago: American Library Association/Resources and Technical Services Division, 1989.

OCLC/AMIGOS. *Collection Analysis CD*. Dallas: AMIGOS, 1989. [This is a computer-based database on a CD-ROM disk constructed individually for libraries who wish to compare their collections with those of peer institutions. One subscribes to periodic updates to the initial database.]

Shoemaker, Sarah. *Collection Management: Current Issues*. New York: Neal-Schuman Publishers, 1989.

Slote, Stanley. *Weeding Library Collections*, 3d ed. Littleton, CO: Libraries Unlimited, 1990.

Stueart, Robert D. and George B. Miner. *Collection Development in Libraries: A Treatise*. 2 volumes. Greenwich, CT: JAI Press, 1980.

— 4 —

Preservation Management

Introduction and Definition

A wide range of literature dealing with preservation reflects the acute concern with the condition of library collections deteriorating all over the world, and growing realization that the responsibility for meeting the "preservation challenge" rests foremost with the librarians in each institution. Terminology has not been standardized, but the term "preservation" is used today to cover all activities involving the maintenance of a library collection in a usable state for as long as needed. The term "conservation" denotes the technical activities of repairing and restoring damaged library material. A more detailed definition by the American Library Association describes preservation as "A broad range of activities intended to extend the life of deteriorating library materials or to retain the intellectual content of deteriorated or embrittled materials. Preservation includes selection of replacement copies, identification of items for retention in storage or protected access, and the selection of materials for conversion to alternate formats such as microforms."[1]

Today many major academic and research libraries have established the position of "library conservator" (or a similar title) for a person who is in overall charge of preservation management of large and important collections. Medium-sized public and academic libraries may lack the resources for such a position. Besides, the goals and objectives of smaller libraries focus primarily on current use and not on research-oriented longevity of their holdings. In these libraries, preservation management, being concerned with collection maintenance, often falls within the area of technical services. However, the consensus is that preservation rests on an awareness and attitude that should be integrated into all library functions and services. As libraries struggle to stretch their budgets while maintaining their collections in serviceable condition for as long as needed, preservation becomes an important part of sound fiscal responsibility. Professional education in library schools should provide a basic understanding of the concepts, issues, and currently available solutions and options concerning preservation. In addition, technical services administrators should encourage and provide continuing education and training opportunities for library staff through attendance at workshops, conferences, etc. There also are excellent audiovisual programs available for staff training. A very good beginning is the film *Slow Fires*, which raises general preservation awareness both among the staff and library constituents.

Preservation Problems

To understand preservation problems, librarians need to know the basic properties of the library/media materials in their care, and the causes for their deterioration, which have been covered well in the literature. Materials in libraries consist mostly of paper, cloth, leather, and audiovisual media. Three major kinds of damage have been identified:

1. Physical damage

   • heat and humidity (especially fluctuations in temperature and relative humidity)
   • water damage (from floods, plumbing failures, fires)
   • light damage (ultraviolet radiation from exposure to sun and fluorescent lights)

2. Chemical deterioration

 • air pollution
 • acid paper (from alum and lignin in wood; residual bleaches; poor ink quality); all destroy cellulose fibers

3. Biological damage

 • insects
 • rodents
 • fungi (e.g. mold)
 • people (users, librarians, binders, etc.)[2]

These kinds of damage to library materials have a cumulative effect. Paper produced since the Industrial Revolution in the mid-nineteenth century, when wood pulp was introduced to meet increased demand, contains components that result in chemical deterioration. It becomes brittle and self-destructs, a process that is exacerbated by being exposed to the effects of air pollution. All materials, of course, are subject to normal wear and tear.

Preservation Planning

Technical services library administrators have to deal with two basic aspects in preservation: retrospective preservation and preventive preservation measures.

RETROSPECTIVE PRESERVATION

This involves the care of deteriorating library material, which may be in such poor physical condition that it is no longer safe to handle. Responsible decisions have to be made about whether to replace, reformat, discard, or repair the damaged material. These decisions are based on such factors as the policy of an institution which covers current and long-range plans for collection development. Rare and special materials should be taken care of by a professional custodian who is in charge of such collections, but this chapter is mainly concerned with the general collection. Collection development policies will differ functionally between public and academic libraries according to their respective mission statements and goals. To be considered in the context of preservation concerns are any resource-sharing activities between institutions or through network agreements.

As a first step, the staff has to decide whether an item is still needed in the active collection, and has not been outdated by later editions, etc. After such a decision, the librarian has several options: to replace; to reformat; to repair; or to discard.

Replacement. If an item is still in print, a replacement can be ordered. If out-of-print, the reprint and antiquarian market can be explored quickly, or reformatting considered.

Reformatting. If the item in itself has no artifactual or intrinsic value (which is usually the case with items from the general collections), but its intellectual content/information should be preserved and no replacement is available, transfer of the content to another format can be considered. First, bibliographic sources should be searched to determine whether a reformatting for this item has already been done by another institution or by a commercial reprinter, and whether a photocopy or microfilm copy is available. Microfilming for preservation purposes (usually called "preservation microfilming") today is considered the most acceptable and cost-effective method of reformatting. Promising technologies are on the horizon, but as yet are not sufficiently tested and standardized to replace microfilming on a large scale and as an affordable alternative. An important consideration for the librarian is the choice of a reputable vendor for preservation microfilming, one who adheres to high standards and offers a good contract. There are many good services available, both from regional centers such as the Northeast Document Conservation Center in Andover, Massachusetts, and a number of commercial firms. Librarians should visit such facilities and gain a clear understanding of the process and quality control used by a vendor.

Repair. Many libraries have set up some kind of in-house facility for carrying out simple repair of items from the general collection. It cannot be emphasized enough that librarians should never attempt to perform themselves any repair on rare and valuable library material, but allow only professional conservators to handle such material. Good advice for librarians is: If in doubt, do NOT touch the material, but consult first with a professional conservator. Much damage has been done to material by well-meaning librarians. However, simple repairs can be done in a library for material that has no permanent value, but still needs to be used. Facilities could be set up for simple cleaning, mending, encapsulation,[3] and the use of other protective enclosures. So-called "phase boxes" are available from the Northeast Document Conservation Center and commercial library binders. They provide a protective enclosure for a damaged item which is still important to the collection, but for whose restoration funds currently are not available.

Discard. If an item having no artifactual or intrinsic value is in such a condition that it is no longer usable, and if the information it contains is no longer needed, or if its contents are available from other institutions either through interlibrary loan or in a reformatted manifestation, removal from the collection is advisable.

PREVENTIVE PRESERVATION MEASURES

Today preventive measures to avoid long-term damage and the effects of disasters are considered a first priority for all types of libraries. They are of great importance to middle-sized academic and public libraries because of their potential to have a significant impact. First on the list of preventive measures is environmental control. Three components in a program of environmental control include keeping air pollution at a minimum (e.g. through use of air conditioning with filtering systems); keeping temperature and relative humidity (RH) constant and protecting material from exposure to ultraviolet light and radiation. If air conditioning is not available, room-type humidifiers and dehumidifiers can be used, depending on the season. Some recommended figures for temperature and humidity are 65–68 degrees Fahrenheit and

45–50 percent relative humidity. The recommended storage control for various types of nonbook material is even lower. There are protective plastic sleeves available to put over light fixtures, or they can be treated with protective varnishes. Windows can be double-glazed or shades or curtains can be added to screen out unwanted light rays.

Secondly, housekeeping and building maintenance can be employed to help preserve materials. Librarians should have the physical plant inspected regularly, especially the roof, attic, and cellars as well as all rooms in the library building, for any leaks or other damage. The library, especially the stacks, should be kept clean and free of food or other waste particles that could invite infestations.

Third, good storage procedures and proper handling of library materials can help. The physical environment, including condition of rooms and appropriate shelving, should meet recommended standards for different types of library material. The library staff has to be trained in the proper handling of material, so that they can set an example for users and instruct them when required. A number of printed and audiovisual guidelines are available to show proper shelving procedures so as not to damage the bindings, how to remove books from the shelves without causing damage to the spine, how to stack them correctly, etc. Audiovisuals can be of great help in educating the staff and the public, and some do it in a rather entertaining way. Much damage can be done to bound material, especially to the bindings, when they are thrown into book drops or forced to lie flat for copying. The use of book drops should be minimized, for example, they should not be used when the library is open. New preservation-conscious copying machines are now on the market which do not require pressure on books.

Fourth, libraries can protect the security of library material. Libraries need to have a written policy for the use of each type of material in their collection to help the staff in supervising its use and circulation. Appropriate steps should be taken to protect the collection from vandalism and theft, either through a mechanical security system or the employment of guards, depending on the situation. There are very useful guidelines available to help libraries select the system best suited to their needs.

Conducting a survey of preservation needs is a fifth way to prevent damage to materials. Preceding any preservation planning, a professional survey should examine the physical facilities and assess the condition of the collection, resulting in recommendations for appropriate action and setting of priorities. Although guidelines for conducting such a survey and sufficient publications are available to make it possible for librarians to learn how to do this themselves, it is even better if the survey can be carried out by an outside professional. The survey report should include a description and evaluation of the building and rooms for suitability as repositories for library materials; an assessment of the condition of the general collection and recommendations for remedial action, if required; suggested priorities and estimated costs; and an indication of what can be done in-house. This report will give the librarian support for implementing preservation measures, and thus serve as an important document for preservation planning and for generating financial support. There may be subsidies available to libraries who contact a regional center, such as the Northeast Document Conservation Center, to perform a survey.

Sixth, emergency planning and disaster preparedness can prove invaluable in the event of a catastrophic event. One of the single most important steps the technical services department can take is to recommend preparation of a contingency plan in order to minimize the damage and speed up recovery. Librarians who have not started in this direction disregard one of their most important responsibilities—taking proper care of the collections in their custody. There are a number of excellent guidelines, workbooks, and other helpful publications for the various types of libraries, but they need to be adapted to the unique situation in each institution. The disaster preparedness and recovery plan for an institution should be based on the survey report. The disaster plan should have input from all departments of a library and be re-examined yearly in order to meet changing needs.

Finally, materials with longer life expectation can be produced using new technologies that address problems of paper and bindings. The new paper standard recommends the use of alkaline paper and is expected to improve the quality of book paper by reducing acidity and ensuring durable properties.[5] University presses have begun printing on alkaline paper and major trade publishers are committed to print the first run of trade publications on such paper whenever possible. Eventually, brittle paper will be less of a problem for libraries. Technical services librarians should check incoming publications for the infinity symbol indicating that the paper meets the new standards.

A new binding standard was published in 1986 by the Library Binding Institute, and four years later, the American Library Association issued a useful interpretation of the standard.[6] Technical services librarians need to know the basics of evaluating the quality of bindings and should keep in close contact with their library binder to be up-to-date on current developments in the field and the types of bindings available. A good library binder will work with the technical services librarian and offer advice according to a library's needs and budget.

Organizing for Preservation Management

Guidelines for a suggested organization for preservation management developed by George M. Cunha can still be adopted today:

• Appoint a staff member who will be responsible for preservation management, one closely connected with the general management of the collection, thus a member of the technical services staff.
• Define the responsibility and authority of this staff member, and the person(s) to whom she/he reports with her/his recommendations. Technical services administrators should be very supportive of the designated staff member and any reasonable recommendations for preservation measures. The

preservation staff member should further be given the following charges:

• Assemble a preservation reference collection for technical services with access for all staff members of the library. This collection should provide guidance and instruction to the staff.

• Include a report on preservation as a regular agenda item at staff meetings.

• Give regular instruction to staff and encourage their continuing education activities in preservation through seminars, workshops, conferences, etc.

• Correct unsatisfactory practices of staff in handling library material and reinforce sound practices.

• Monitor regularly HVAC (heating/ventilation/air-conditioning) systems, temperature, humidity, air pollution, lighting, housekeeping, pest control, and recommend corrective measures.

• Prepare budget estimates for preservation and include preservation components in the regular budget.

• Plan emergency and security policy and monitor appropriate equipment to safeguard holdings from fire and other disasters.

• Cooperate with other institutions in solving common preservation problems.[7]

Summary and Recommendations

Once preservation has become a regular component of technical services functions, it needs to be integrated into all library activities affecting the handling, storage, evaluation, and use of library material. In libraries where the top management is preservation conscious, this will be carried out easily from the top level down. Otherwise, the technical services staff may have to make every effort to promote preservation convincingly to the director and throughout the library. The preparation of a written preservation policy is highly recommended, either as part of a collection management policy or a collection maintenance policy.

Preservation awareness is a continuous effort and the costs of a good program may be a serious problem. However, over the long run, preventing serious damage to large numbers of materials is less costly than repairs to the same number of materials would be. The cost of preservation measures should be weighed against the savings they provide in extending the useful life of library materials. Preservation resource sharing by all types of libraries probably will become increasingly important, and will involve sharing preservation materials, equipment, and expertise.

Preservation in the Surveyed Libraries

Most libraries in the survey reported some preservation activities in the areas of processing and binding. Forty-two (out of sixty-one) had some in-house operation; nineteen had a separate bindery unit, both preparing material for binding and carrying out actual bindings; fifty-seven libraries performed in-house mending and repairs; forty-two libraries put protective coverings and some reinforcing dust covers on material; thirty-seven libraries had inserted security devices in material. Thirty-three libraries reported a separate unit for processing material for binding. In other cases binding preparation and processing were integrated with other units of the library. Only one, a university library, reported a separate preservation unit. As to the staff performing these activities, four reported employing trained conservators (two volunteers), and two paraprofessionals. Comments made by respondents included the following:

"Book repair to be handled by various library departments."

"Mending mainly of juvenile books."

"A single volunteer is responsible for mending of materials. If the material is bad enough to be sent to the bindery, then the Public Services Librarian makes the decision, which is sent, or replaced, or discarded."

"Binding is done in Technical Services. Minor book repairs are handled in the Circulation Unit—usually by students."

The survey showed an alarming lack of any preservation policy or systematic planning for preservation. In most cases in-house repairs and mending are performed by volunteers without indication that they had proper instruction and supervision. There seems to be a great need for the technical services staff and library management to become informed of preservation issues as discussed above, and to develop a productive preservation plan for their libraries.

A Selective Reference Collection
for Preservation Management

The following is a suggested reference collection for the library staff.

1. ARTICLES AND MONOGRAPHS

American National Standards Institute. *American National Standard for Information Sciences—Permanence of Paper for Printed Library Materials*. Washington: ANSI, 1984. (American National Standards for Information Sciences, ISSN 8756 0860; Z39.48–1984).

Association of Research Libraries (ARL). Although aimed primarily at the large academic and research libraries, ARL and its Office of Management Services (OMS) have a very useful preservation publications program, including audiovisuals and pertinent guidelines. Information can be obtained from the Association of Research Libraries, 1527 New Hampshire Avenue, NW, Washington, DC 20036.

Barton, John P. and Johanna G. Wellheiser, eds. *An Ounce of Prevention: A Handbook on Disaster Contingency Planning for Archives, Libraries and Record Centres*. Toronto: Toronto Area Archivists Group Education Foundation, 1985.

Bohem, Hilda. *Disaster Prevention and Disaster Preparedness*. Berkeley, CA: Office of the Assistant Vice President, April 1978.

Brand, Marvine, ed. *Security for Libraries, People, Buildings, Collections*. Chicago: American Library Association, 1984.

Buchanan, Sally A. *Disaster Planning, Preparedness and Recovery for Libraries and Archives: A RAMP [Records and Archives Management*

Programme] Study with Guidelines. Paris: UNESCO, 1988. (PGI-88/WS/6)

"A Core Collection in Preservation," compiled by Lisa L. Fox for the Education Committee of the Preservation of Library Materials Section, RTSD, ALA. Chicago: Resources and Technical Services Division, American Library Association, 1988.

Cunha, George Martin and Dorothy Grant Cunha. *Conservation of Library Materials: A Manual and Bibliography on the Care, Repair and Restoration of Library Materials.* 2d ed. 2 vols. Metuchen, NJ: Scarecrow Press, 1971. Volume one still is a classic; volume two (Bibliography) is only of retrospective interest.

————. *Libraries and Archives Conservation: 1980s and Beyond.* 2 vols. Metuchen, NJ: Scarecrow Press, 1983. Volume one is the text; volume two is a bibliography.

Cunha, George M. *Methods of Evaluation to Determine the Preservation Needs in Libraries and Archives: A RAMP Study with Guidelines. Paris: UNESCO, 1988. (PGI-88/WS/16)*

Disaster Plan Workbook. Prepared by the Preservation Committee, New York University Libraries, 1983.

England, Claire. *Disaster Management for Libraries: Planning Process.* Toronto: Canadian Library Association, 1988.

Greenfield, Jane. *Books: Their Care and Repair.* New York: H.W. Wilson, 1983.

Gwinn, Nancy E., ed. *Preservation Microfilming: A Guide for Librarians and Archivists.* Chicago: American Library Association, 1987. The definitive publication on the topic.

Horton, Carolyn. *Cleaning and Preserving Bindings and Related Materials.* 2d rev. ed. Chicago: American Library Association, 1969.

Kyle, Hedi. *Library Materials Preservation Manual: Practical Methods for Preserving Books, Pamphlets and Other Printed Materials.* Bronxville, NY: Nicholas T. Smith, 1983.

Lowry, Marcia Duncan. "Preservation and Conservation in the Small Library." Chicago: Library Administration and Management Association, American Library Association, 1989. (Small Libraries Publications, no. 15).

Merrill-Oldham, Jan. "Preservation Comes of Age: An Action Agenda for the '80s and Beyond." *American Libraries* (Dec. 1985): 770–72.

Morris, John. *Library Disaster Preparedness Handbook.* Chicago: American Library Association, 1986.

Morrow, Carolyn Clark and Carole Dyal. *Conservation Treatment Procedures*. 2d ed. Littleton, CO: Libraries Unlimited, 1986.

Morrow, Carolyn Clark, with Gay Walker. *The Preservation Challenge: A Guide to Conserving Library Materials*. White Plains, NY: Knowledge Industries, 1983. Now available from G.K. Hall, Boston, MA.

O'Connell, Mildred. "Disaster Planning: Writing and Implementing Plans for Collections-holding Institutions." *Technology and Conservation* 2 (1983): 18–24.

Parisi, Paul A. "Methods of Affixing Leaves: Options and Implications." *New Library Scene* (1983): 9–12.

Pinion, Catherine F. "Preservation of Audiovisual Materials (Unesco Seminar, Berlin, May 1987)." *IFLA Journal* 13 (1987): 402–04.

The Standard for Library Binding. 8th ed., edited by Paul A. Parisi and Jan Merrill-Oldham. Rochester, NY: Library Binding Institute, 1986. The *Standard* is being interpreted to librarians by Jan Merrill-Oldham and Paul Parisi in *A Guide to The Library Institute Standard for Library Binding*. Chicago: American Library Association, 1990.

Swartzburg, Susan G. *Conservation in the Library: A Handbook on the Use and Care of Traditional and Nontraditional Materials*. Westport, CT: Greenwood Press, 1983.

───────. *Preserving Library Materials: A Manual*. Metuchen, NJ: Scarecrow Press, 1980.

Waters, Peter. *Emergency Procedures for Salvage of Water-Damaged Materials*. 2d ed. Washington: Library of Congress, 1979. A standard component of disaster plans.

Williams, B.J.S. "Implications for Preservation of the Newer Information Media." *Media and Technology* 19 (1986): 15.

2. JOURNALS

The Abbey Newsletter (6/year)

Conservation Administration News (*CAN*) (4/year)

Library and Archival Security (4/year)

New Library Scene (formerly *Library Scene*), and other library journals, such as

Library Resources & Technical Services (official journal of the Association for Library Collections and Technical Services, American Library Association).

Cataloging, Classification, and Indexing

Organizing library materials so that someone can identify a desired item quickly and easily from among the thousands of titles in the collection is the purpose of cataloging, classification, and indexing. These operations are the responsibility of the catalog department, which always has been central to technical services.

Librarians organize materials in two ways: (1) they arrange them on the shelves in groups that bring together items on the same or related topics; and (2) they prepare lists or catalogs of the holdings that can be searched for a desired item so patrons need not go to the shelves and examine each item there. Both of these organizational strategies—creating topical shelf arrangements through classification and creating lists of surrogates for each title in the collection through descriptive cataloging and indexing—facilitate access for the people who use libraries.

Historical Background

Before 1900, every library was on its own. Catalog librarians in each library received every new item that passed through the acquisitions department and cataloged, classified, and indexed it (i.e., assigned subject headings to it). Large libraries prepared printed book catalogs from time to time, and kept records for materials acquired between editions by printing on slips or in handwritten ledgers. The printed books were valuable as reference tools, and useful in attracting donors of valuable materials, whose names might be perpetuated in future editions if they contributed their collections to the library. Libraries without the funds to have their catalogs printed could keep handwritten lists of their holdings.

After 1900, when the Library of Congress (LC) began to sell its printed catalog cards, the card file gained immediate popularity. It was easy to keep up to date, very hospitable to new entries, and less costly to maintain than printed books or handwritten lists. Libraries had the option of buying LC's cards for newly acquired items when the cards were available; but they still had to catalog, classify, and index those items for which LC cards were not available. Thus, cataloging departments tended to have many highly skilled, professionally educated and trained librarians who devoted their careers to cataloging, classifying, and creating catalog records for materials as well as directing a large group of support staff in carrying out the tasks of precataloging, verifying, typing, duplicating, filing, and maintaining the library's catalogs.

Then, as now, libraries maintained at least two catalogs: a dictionary catalog in which records are retrievable by author, title, and subject; and a shelflist, i.e., a catalog arranged in shelf order (in other words, by call number). The shelflist, a classified catalog, rarely was available in public areas. It was the place where inventory information about individual copies of titles was recorded and used by staff members in keeping track of the acquisition, costs, and eventual de-acquisition of the library's stock. The dictionary catalog, intended for public use, was a catalog in which the author, title, and subject records for each title in the collection were arranged alphabetically—a preference generally attributed to Charles A. Cutter.[1] The dictionary catalog was and still is referred to as the public catalog, since it is a prominent fixture in the public area of the library, and is the means whereby members of the public find bibliographic information about items in the collection.

Years ago, it was not unusual for libraries to have four or five separate catalogs: a public catalog which might be divided into two files, an author-title file and a subject file; a serials catalog giving specific information about serials holdings; an "official" catalog (a staff-only file); and a shelflist. The official catalog was a duplicate of the public catalog with two critical differences: each title had only one entry, almost always the main entry; and the filing was always kept up-to-date. The latter was extremely important, since filing in the public catalog could lag by weeks or months. Libraries also might have separate catalogs for audiovisual materials, microform copies of books and serials, and the holdings of particular departments, branches, or subject areas. It was not unusual for library systems made up of a central library and branches or groups of separate libraries to have, in addition, a separate union list, although just as often there might be none, or the main library's shelflist might serve as the only combined list of materials.

From 1900 onward, the catalogs themselves were almost always in the form of card files, although a few libraries kept the printed book catalogs popular in earlier days, supplemented by slips, lists, or card files for titles cataloged between printings. Cataloging work was time-consuming and labor-intensive, and catalogers were kept busy creating and maintaining the records for all of the different files.

The Bibliographic Utilities
and the Rise of Copy Cataloging

Since the 1970s, work in cataloging departments has changed in fundamental ways as a result of the advent of computerized networks of shared bibliographic records, called bibliographic utilities, and computer-based catalogs, called online public access catalogs (OPACs). All computer-based catalogs are known as OPACs whether they actually are online with a dynamic, interactive, real-time, online cataloging system or merely connected to a static, offline database on a CD-ROM disk, as described briefly in Chapter 2.

When computerized catalog records for the bulk of the materials one purchases are found in an online bibliographic network or utility such as OCLC, RLIN, or WLN, cataloging librarians do not have to create records for any but the items not found in the database. For some libraries the small group of items for which records cannot be found might be as little as one percent of their total acquisitions. What remains to be done, and what occupies cataloging departments that use bibliographic utilities, is finding and adjusting the network records to conform to local policies and practices, and supervising the maintenance of local catalogs.

The process of adjusting network records to local practice, called editing or copy cataloging, consists of four basic steps:

1. Finding a computerized record that matches the item in hand;
2. Correcting any information that does not match exactly or that appears to be incorrect;
3. Adding missing information and local information, such as a local call number or a note referring solely to the library's copy; and,
4. Punching in a command to add the library's holdings symbol to the record in the database, and to produce cards or catalog records in other media for the library's catalog and/or a permanent record called an archival record of the transaction on magnetic tape.

Libraries that have eliminated their manual catalogs and replaced them with OPACs do not want their catalog records on cards. They want to receive their cataloging on magnetic tapes, disks, or cassettes that can be loaded into the OPAC's database; or they may have hardware and software that enables the edited records from the utility to be passed directly into the OPAC's database from the bibliographic utility without external disks, tapes, or other kinds of storage equipment.

Editing existing records, even though it actually requires

fairly sophisticated bibliographic knowledge, is not a very challenging process compared to cataloging items from scratch. It does require good computer search skills, excellent data processing skills, and sharp eyes for accuracy. There are many more data elements in a standard computerized record than there are on a card-style record and certain keystrokes can be critical. Computer filing is literal and exact, and, unless it is specially programmed to do so, a computer cannot be expected to recognize and accommodate such common errors as transposed letters or numbers, erroneous singular or plural words, incorrectly entered punctuation, etc. Thus, in addition to having certain knowledge of cataloging, classification and indexing, copy catalogers must know how to operate the computer systems and input data into them correctly, rapidly, and accurately.

The reason there are more fields in a standard computerized catalog record than on a catalog card is because the MARC computer communications format used by all the bibliographic utilities and major vendors of computer-based cataloging systems contains a great variety of control fields wanted by LC, MARC's originator. MARC records were designed to contain all the data that appeared on LC cards and more, since some of the control fields include coded versions of eye-readable data appearing elsewhere and some of the fields were needed to enable programmers to utilize LC's existing or proposed hardware and system software. Other fields were included but not defined, with a view toward utilizing them in the future. The paradigm on which the MARC format is based appears to be the LC printed card, even though certain fields at the beginning of the MARC record (e.g., the LC catalog card number and the ISBN) are printed at the bottom of the cards.

For the most part, a library's entrance into a bibliographic utility has been accompanied by shrinking the number of professionally educated cataloging librarians and turning the major portion of work in the cataloging department over to paraprofessional copy catalogers. In larger libraries and even in many medium-sized libraries, cataloging departments which had never been divided or which were divided by subject or language, now were divided into original and copy cataloging units, with the latter containing the lion's share of the staff and doing the overwhelming majority of the work.

Even the supporting paraprofessional staff have been affected by the computer revolution in cataloging. Libraries that also have implemented OPACs no longer require the services of armies of filers and revisers to enter finished catalog records into the file or to remove records for discarded materials. Instead, initial filing is done automatically, and removal or revision of records is done by data entry staff called keyboarders. Eventually, even the keyboarders may be replaced by more sophisticated input/output-devices-plus-software that will be able to recognize wanted changes and make them simply by passing an appropriately marked title page under a scanner.

Three major issues have emerged as a result of the computerization of cataloging and the rise of shared cataloging networks:

1. The amount of editing local libraries should do to the records they find in bibliographic utilities;
2. The reorganization of personnel and workflow in cataloging departments;
3. The integration of cataloging work and bibliographic files (such as the catalog and shelflist) with other library files, services, and systems.

In the next sections, these issues are explored in greater detail.

To Edit or Not to Edit . . .

THE PURPOSES AND COSTS OF EDITING

The initial purposes of OCLC, the first U.S. bibliographic utility, were to speed up the cataloging process as well as to lower its cost. Certain uses of the bibliographic database created through OCLC's system of shared cataloging, such as resource sharing, were envisioned at the start but given lower priorities, while knowledge of other uses developed along with the system. The main idea was to find a network record and use it, without change or with as little change as possible, for one's local catalog. As a result, policies and strategies to build the database quickly were employed, e.g., the library that puts in a record for the first time receives a small financial reward not given to those who use someone else's record.

In the early years of OCLC's OnLine Union Catalog (OLUC), the largest proportion of records originated at LC, whose products set the national standard for excellence. MARC tapes containing all cataloging done at LC were purchased by OCLC and loaded into the OLUC. The system was programmed to replace a member-contributed record with a matching record from LC. Thus, librarians assumed that most of the records they used would come from LC's MARC database, providing them with the same high quality data found on printed cards, only faster. This assumption was true, however, only for the first few years of network operation. The number of non-LC records contributed by network members grew ever more rapidly as OCLC's membership grew, first to colleges outside the state of Ohio and later to non-academic libraries throughout the United States and the world. Eventually the balance tipped in favor of member-contributed cataloging and the proportion of LC records has diminished steadily since then. RLIN avoided this problem. Unlike OCLC, in which each item cataloged is represented by one master record, the RLIN database was designed to retain all catalog records entered, with multiple records for an item being clustered for retrieval. One's own records or the records of any other library can be called up, giving copy catalogers many more possibilities from which to select a record to edit.

Maintenance of cataloging quality in OCLC and later in RLIN relied on the self discipline of member libraries, who had to agree to follow national cataloging standards for the records they contributed, and to identify the fullness of records according to network input standards. Another assumption made in the early years of shared network cataloging that was short-lived was that all contributors to the database were equally capable of doing high quality cataloging. In practice it was not true, and both OCLC and RLIN catalog records are likely to contain errors of various kinds.[2]

During the decade of the 1970s, several developments exacerbated cataloging debates as they intensified. Some academic libraries that had used the Dewey Decimal classification (DDC) until their entrance into a bibliographic utility then switched to the Library of Congress classification (LCC) to take advantage of the larger number of LCC call numbers available in network records. They were faced with the need to reclassify their existing collections as well as to use a new classification system for materials that did not have records available online. In 1978, publication of the second edition of the *Anglo-American Cataloguing Rules* (*AACR2*), the nation's standard for descriptive cataloging, not only changed the rules for many parts of the catalog description, but altered the way headings were created for whole categories of names. These rule changes required rebuilding name authorities from scratch for the changed names and filing them differently than the older heading versions. For example, Lewis Carroll, who had been filed in the "D"s as "Dodgson, Charles Lutwidge" before *AACR2*, was changed to "Carroll, Lewis," and filed in the "C"s; and all the state universities with "University of ****" names, which had been filed as "****. University." under the initial letters of their state names, now were known as "University of ****" and filed in the "U"s.

With the implementation of *AACR2*, which was delayed at LC and the bibliographic utilities until January 1, 1981 to help the research library community prepare for it, a new conflict arose over how best to deal with the catalog. Libraries could maintain two public catalogs, closing the old one in which the old rules were followed and beginning a new one in which the new rules were followed; or they could interfile all records in one catalog leaving the old records alone, adding new records with new headings, and linking the files thus split with cross references; or they could update the old records in part or in full, so all the records in one unified catalog would be more or less consistent. Librarians adopted the phrase "retrospective conversion" to refer to the conversion of pre-AACR2 headings to AACR2 style and/or the reclassification of materials from DDC to LCC nearly as often as they used it to refer to the conversion of manual catalog records to computerized forms.

In order to benefit most from shared network cataloging in terms of the time it takes to prepare a catalog record and the unit cost of the local catalog record, editing must be kept at a minimum. Yet for catalog librarians accustomed to the accuracy and fullness of LC-style records, extensive editing of records found online seemed the only way to maintain the quality and integrity of their local catalogs. The conflict between these objectives, i.e., speed and cost versus accuracy and fullness, has created problems and tensions within catalog departments as well as between catalog departments and other units of the library and/or its administration.

There has been no single resolution to the question of how much to edit. Individual catalog managers have to arrive at an equilibrium as best they can, somewhere on a continuum between no editing and comprehensive editing, given their workloads and resources, and considering the needs of their clientele. Generally speaking, professionally educated cataloging librarians have argued for more editing of online records to keep the quality of online cataloging at least equal to their previous manual procedures; but library directors, seeing their budgets shrink from a combination of funding cuts, inflation, and heavier demands on collections and services, angrily argue against it. After all, directors rightfully claim, online cataloging was supposed to lower costs and speed up processes, and editing detracts from both.

In some libraries, the editing conflict goes on, but in others, directors beat the opposition by eliminating them, either by attrition or by reassigning the professionally educated librarians to other departments and filling the positions with non-degreed staff whose expertise was in data processing, particularly keyboarding.[3] An unforeseen result has been a shortage of catalogers attributed by many to the erroneous belief that this specialty is no longer needed.[4]

EDITING TOOLS

One might think that many editing tools would spring up to assist copy catalogers in their work, but this has not been the case. The principal tools for editing are aids provided by the network, e.g., the capability of doing full-screen editing,[5] lists and directories of necessary codes and symbols, input standards, and other documentation. Similar to most computer documentation, these aids often are written in computerese or networkese, and they are difficult to understand and to use. LC publishes the official version of the MARC format, and some networks require that it be used to supplement their documentation.

The first and most important tool one might wish to have is a guide to efficient searching, particularly for systems (such as OCLC's) that do not permit full names and titles to be entered as search requests. A few such aids do exist, including a periodically updated guide to searching and a briefer "ref-card" supplied free of charge by OCLC,[6] but this type of tool does not seem to be very popular. Instead, new copy catalogers may be taught the basics of searching by a colleague, a supervisor, or a professionally educated cataloger and then be left to experiment and develop their skills on their own.

Much editing is done directly on-screen by a copy cataloger holding the item being processed in hand. When this is the procedure, few checks on editing quality are possible, although the edited records may be saved in a temporary file for checking and approval before being uploaded to the network database. In some places, however, editing is done using a paper counterpart of a blank online record called a worksheet. The worksheet mimics the computer screen version of the MARC format with a few differences, e.g., infrequently used fields may be omitted and frequently encountered data may be pre-entered. Spaces to be filled in are more clearly marked on a worksheet than on the screen, and occasionally explanations or field mnemonics are added. Corrections and additions may be entered on the worksheet, and be checked and approved by a supervisor before being entered into the database.

A useful tool for copy catalogers would be an up-to-date set of conversion tables between LCC and DDC. With such a tool, it would not make any difference what type of call number was found in the online record. Conversion tables were published in the 1970s, when libraries were switching from Dewey to LC classification,[7] but they have not been kept current. Classification is one of the most difficult jobs copy catalogers face, yet there is very little supporting documentation to help make it easier.

Another useful tool for copy catalogers would be a manual or, even better, an online help file containing assistance with commonly encountered editing data, e.g., a list of abbreviated publisher's names, a list of appropriate language abbreviations for non-English and multilingual works with codes for the corresponding control field, a list of codes for the control field one uses when the subject heading contains a geographic name, etc. A copy cataloger's cataloging manual might contain alternate methods of recording date of publication, distribution, etc., and the corresponding control field when one has multiple dates or a guessed date. These tricky situations are spelled out in great detail in the rules of *AACR2* as well as in network documentation, but sometimes they are difficult to grasp if one has not spent a semester or two in a formal class learning how to read them.

The best editing support outside the individual library might be expected to come from the networks, and many if not all of their regional affiliates offer workshops on MARC coding and tagging on a regular basis. OCLC has even begun offering cataloging workshops, particularly for materials other than books, e.g., serials, audiovisual materials, computer files, etc. Training within the individual library for copy catalogers is even more critical in maximizing the institution's benefits from network participation, since only it can include emphasis on elements in the process that are of importance in the local situation.

EDITING POLICIES

Every library that uses a network database and edits records found online should have a written editing policy. A policy document stating the goals and objectives of the library with regard to use of the network database and provision of local catalog records is the basis for all local practice, and individual procedures should flow from the overall goals and objectives. Unfortunately, in some libraries editing policies are still passed orally from one cataloger to another, risking the possibility of misstating or misunderstanding on the part of the speaker and the listener. Sometimes the errors do not surface for a long time, while hundreds of records are processed incorrectly; occasionally the errors never surface or cannot be explained, and are never corrected systematically.

Arlene Taylor's *Cataloging with Copy: A Decision-Maker's Handbook*[8] is the principal guide to editing policymaking available. It describes the process of editing, the decisions that should be considered, and outlines alternative practices and the results that can be expected from each one.

As the network, cataloging, and library environments change, editing policies and procedures need attention to be sure they reflect current modes of thinking as well as current needs and system capabilities. Advances in computing and related technologies are occurring rapidly and having direct and indirect effects on the world of information production and distribution as well as on bibliographic networks, cataloging rules, and local library computer systems. Success in the search for expert systems that can produce cataloging automatically from a scan of a title page or other data source may eventually obviate the need for editing entirely.

Staff and Workflow Reorganization

Some of the results of computerizing cataloging operations and catalog products that were largely unforeseen were changes in staffing needs and workflow that began quietly, but rapidly became far-reaching and radical in nature. Among the factors that drove the changes were the deprofessionalization of cataloging operations and the distributed processing capabilities of new computer systems. Both of these gave public service librarians opportunities for and interests in cataloging decision making that would have been unthinkable in earlier days. As this chapter is being written, a new paradigm for bibliographic services seems to be emerging, although it is by no means clear that other developments cannot or will not occur.

THE DEPROFESSIONALIZATION OF CATALOGING

Before the days of network databases and library computing, the cataloging department consisted of large numbers of professionally educated and trained librarians. In those days, every book acquired needed their attention. Since the advent of computerized cataloging, the numbers of professional catalogers employed solely in cataloging departments have dwindled steadily, replaced by computer terminals manned by copy catalogers without library school degrees. Reviewing this evolution of cataloging staff, it would seem clear that deprofessionalization has occurred, at least insofar as sheer numbers are concerned. But other factors may be seen to be at work if one looks beyond the library's own in-house cataloging department to the totality of cataloging production.

In the first place, bibliographic networks employ large numbers of cataloging personnel, since cataloging is a primary module of every network. These experts do not sit at desks and catalog materials. They perform a host of duties associated with network activity, including working with hardware and software staff on improvements to the database, operating internal and external quality control programs, training users in working with new products, conducting research, and interacting with member librarians in other roles. In the second place, computer system vendors also employ staff with cataloging expertise in all areas of their operations, from system design and marketing to training and other user support. Opportunities for cataloging experts outside of libraries have increased and, among these employers, competition for well educated and trained personnel has been keen.

In the third place, libraries also are employing staff with cataloging expertise in different capacities, e.g., as database managers, heads of computer departments, heads of copy cataloging departments, staff trainers, general managers, etc. Catalogers with special expertise in a language, subject, type of material, or audience have been assigned part-time to original cataloging for specialty materials not found in network databases and part-time to other duties that require their expertise, including selecting materials for those parts of the collection, conducting bibliographic research, and giving direct assistance to members of the public.

The ultimate deprofessionalization of cataloging is seen by some as a scenario in which computer hardware and software is designed to scan the bibliographic data of purchased items and translate them automatically into catalog records complete with subject headings and classification numbers. However, substituting a machine-based expert system for the human experts on whom libraries have relied in the past does not deprofessionalize the cataloging, but transfers it to another venue—that of the computer system. What bibliographic computing has done to cataloging is to reveal those tasks among the totality of cataloging tasks that can be reduced to simple yes-no decisions that anyone (or anything) can make, and, by breaking down complex decisions into their component parts, to increase the number of simple decisions that go into cataloging.

Cataloging departments currently tend to have fewer degreed catalogers and more support staff than in pre-computing days. There remain tasks in the cataloging department, however, that can best be performed by degreed librarians who have cataloging expertise. These tasks are primarily managerial in nature, and include recruiting and training copy catalogers; supervising and evaluating their work; planning and supervising departmental budgets, policies, and operations; and interacting with librarians from other departments in the local institution as well as from other institutions. Degreed catalogers are concerning themselves with delivery of bibliographic services, including the catalog as a whole, not with the creation of the individual records that make up the catalogs. Thus, deprofessionalization may be seen as applying to the work of creating catalog records, but not necessarily to the management of bibliographic services.

DISTRIBUTED PROCESSING AND THE PUBLIC
SERVICES LIBRARIAN

Until the advent of computers, bibliographic information in the catalog was confined to the single monolithic card file. If a member of the public, a bibliographer, or a reference librarian assisting a client wished to consult local bibliographic information, they had to go to that one place and look in that one file of bibliographic records. That was it. If one needed some little piece of information to select a desired title, say, the name of a particular editor of a work available in many similar editions, such as a Shakespearean play, and one was off in the stacks, two or three floors and two or three blocks away from the card catalog, one could guess at the correct editor or one could walk all the way back to the catalog and look it up. There were no other choices, since it was difficult to duplicate large card files and extremely costly to house and maintain them.

When computers began to be used for bibliographic data, a fascinating thing happened: once the data was contained in a machine-readable database, it could be searched via any terminal attached to it, either permanently or temporarily. Furthermore, anyone with a keyboard, scanner, or another input/output device attached to the central processing unit could add, edit, or delete data from the database. It was so easy to change data that methods had to be invented to prevent unwanted alteration of data from online catalogs and circulation systems. Passwords and other security checks were furnished to library computers by vendors made keenly aware of the mischief that could be done by the rise of computer crime in the worlds of government and industry.

The significance of the change was that bibliographic processing no longer had to be confined to the single locus of a cataloging department (for input) and a card catalog (for output). People could input data from any terminal, even from an administrator's office, a reference desk, or a branch library, and they could obtain data from any terminal, even from the comfort and privacy of their offices, living rooms, or dormitories. The same terminals could be used for input and output if the library chose, or some terminals could be secured for searching only, or input operations could be secured against unauthorized use. Computerized processing could be distributed, unlike manual processing which had to be centralized.

In the early stages of library computerization, cataloging departments did not pay much attention to the potential of distributed processing. They tended to look at computer terminals as fancier versions of typewriters. As online bibliographic systems have matured, however, two phenomena are occurring:

1. The abilities of public service librarians to contribute their expertise to bibliographic databases have enabled them to assume responsibilities that previously were limited to catalogers;
2. Catalogers can be deployed at public service desks without preventing them from continuing to perform cataloging tasks at these locations.

The result of distributed bibliographic processing appears to be the development of very different perceptions about the most appropriate roles for cataloging and reference librarians, and the rise of dual role positions that include cataloging, bibliography, and direct client service as well as some supervisory or managerial responsibilities.

A new paradigm. James Neal, D. Kaye Gapen, and Maureen Sullivan, current or former library administrators at Indiana University, the University of Wisconsin-Madison, and Yale University respectively, outline a new paradigm for librarians—a paradigm of holistic practitioners using their expertise to do the professional tasks of cataloging *and* public service, not solely one or the other.[9] The key word in this new paradigm is "professional." It implies that the clerical nitty-gritty usually associated with cataloging and reference work will be peeled away from librarians' job descriptions, leaving a nucleus of tasks requiring the special education and expertise of a librarian.

When enumerated, many of the holistic librarian's tasks sound managerial—original cataloging, selection of materials, planning for systems and services, research, designing systems, budgeting, training staff, and making policy—and, in fact, they are. The crucial difference is that, for the first time, the technical service task of original cataloging and the public service task of selecting materials are perceived as having the same central bibliographic component. This is what makes the paradigm new for U.S. libraries in the 1990s, but one could interpret the roles of eighteenth and nineteenth century librarians as being quite similar. Perhaps holistic librarianship is merely a more elaborate reincarnation of what the scholar-librarians of earlier centuries did in managing their much smaller collections and performing all the professional tasks of collecting, organizing, and administering their libraries.

More to the point, the time-consuming, nitty-gritty tasks that usually go with original cataloging (searching databases for entries, verifying name authority records, inputting the resulting bibliographic data, etc.), or that usually go with selecting materials for purchase (checking holdings against bibliographies, obtaining reviews, etc.), will be assigned to non-degreed staff whom the librarians will train and supervise. The new paradigm recognizes that librarians' specialized expertise, gained through their additional education, training, and experience, should not be wasted on tasks that can be done by support staff. It implies that a smaller number of librarians may be able to manage sizeable enterprises, because the work will be organized and divided differently. There also is the possibility that a spinoff benefit for holistic librarians might be higher salaries.

Integrated Bibliographic Systems

THE IDEAL LOCAL SYSTEM

Ideally, local systems might consist of three levels of data:

1. Local data, i.e., bibliographic and inventory data for each local item, whether it is on order, currently held or bor-

rowed, or de-acquisitioned, along with related files such as client data, vendor data, etc.;

2. Data for materials held at other institutions, i.e., union catalogs or access to the catalogs of other libraries;
3. Links to information products, whether or not they are part of the holdings of any particular institution, e.g., Bowker's *Books in Print* database and EBSCO's or FAX-ON's serials database.

Locally controlled item data, an enhanced public catalog including both bibliographic and inventory data for all materials regardless of medium, would be central to each library's system. One advantage of a local database enhanced with acquisition and circulation files is that it can reflect the availability of any item. This type of catalog answers the question, "Can I have this item now?" Another is that it furnishes opportunities for clients to search and request items that have not yet arrived or are otherwise unavailable for browsing. If the database can be searched by call number, it eliminates the need to maintain a separate shelflist. Permanent records held offline and updated periodically, e.g., on CD-ROM disks, might be made for de-accessioned items. This database is useful for reporting purposes at the end of the year (i.e., the records of de-accessioned items for that year) and for reference—a modern variant on the traditional accession file.

Linked with other relevant files such as client files, vendor files, fund files, etc., all technical services functions could be performed through this enhanced system. Linked with full text databases of the contents of materials, the computer terminal could provide its users directly with desired information. It could do this without their having to go to the library in person, wait for service, or encounter delays in obtaining the information they want. While this sort of access to content might not satisfy a music lover's desire to enjoy the Metropolitan Opera's productions of Wagner's *Ring of the Nibelungen*, it might meet a researcher's need to check a fact, copy a quotation, or investigate a book's tables of contents.

The success of an enhanced local system would depend on three factors:

1. Sufficient hardware and computing power to support the desired level of activity;
2. Total conversion of bibliographic, acquisition, and circulation data into the system's database;
3. Powerful, flexible, user-friendly software to facilitate searching and display.

Data for materials held at other institutions, a conglomerate national/international network database, would represent a powerful reference tool. The network would provide a huge secondary pool of materials to which every individual was linked via his or her local library. Needless to add, if the materials in the network database were also available in full text, there would be no waiting for interlibrary loans to arrive by fax or by mail, and the use of all materials might be expected to increase enormously.

Links to information products would provide opportunities to find information not held in library collections but nevertheless potentially useful to library clients. The library could subscribe to all the databases now brokered by DIALOG, BRS, and similar services, as well as to other electronic products of government, commercial, and private producers all over the world.

The ideal system would be a giant universal information center, outdoing even the wildest dreams of twentieth century Universal Bibliographic Control visionaries. Its greatest advantages would be its integration into a single system employing uniform hardware and software, using one set of protocols, and presumably making the most efficient use of data and telecommunications to perform its services.

LINKED *VERSUS* INTEGRATED SYSTEMS

A library can automate its technical services functions in two ways: by having one system capable of doing them all or by having separate systems that may or may not be linked to perform each function. As described in the foregoing section, an integrated system appears to be much better than separate systems, even if they are linked, because it should be simpler to use and it should achieve greater processing efficiency.

Integrated systems having these capabilities and power still are a dream of computing to which librarians might aspire, but which is as yet unavailable.

The reality is that various library computer systems being marketed are only partially integrated, i.e., they may be able to perform more than one function, but none can perform all technical service functions, and only some of them can be linked together. Even more sobering is the cost of moving from older, manual systems to computer-based systems of some size and power, with or without links to multiple systems inside or outside the local library. For virtually all libraries, complete automation is not yet within the foreseeable future. In the meanwhile, they can choose between adding modules to existing computer systems that perform other functions—e.g., adding a cataloging module to a circulation system—or buying separate systems designed to perform specific functions. If one opts for the latter, the systems may or may not be compatible and the development of linkages between or among them may or may not materialize.

LOCAL SYSTEMS AND THE NATIONAL NETWORK

In the early days of library computerization, the expectation was that great central systems similar to the *National Union Catalog* (such as OCLC) would continue to grow larger indefinitely, and local libraries would merely tap into them as members or subscribers. To a certain degree, this notion has not been completely superseded, although it is being challenged. The challenge arose with the introduction of smaller, less costly, but more powerful computers, minicomputers, and powerful microcomputer-based workstations that can do almost as much work as the large mainframe computers of the 1950s. These machines can take advantage of mainframe-produced products to give local libraries enormous computing power at very low prices.

The fact is that locally owned and controlled stand-alone systems based on small minicomputers or enhanced microcomputers now enable all but the largest libraries to do their catalog-related data processing in-house, with or without a direct connection to a bibliographic utility. If they belong to OCLC, RLIN, or WLN, the network serves as a major source of bibliographic data. If not, they can purchase bibliographic databases of varying sizes and contents on CD-ROM disks from commercial vendors such as Gaylord, Marcive, LC, or even from the bibliographic utilities, who now offer a variety of cataloging products derived from their databases.

Local libraries have, once again, the opportunity to attain direct control over their cataloging operations, and the possibility exists that they might begin to resemble the isolated units of pre-1900 years, with the national and international networks generating basic source data primarily from national libraries and major original cataloging institutions. Certainly one would imagine local libraries would welcome having the final say over what their data looks like as well as how much it costs.

Smaller networks have developed among libraries in states, cities, and other local geographic regions, as well as among users of particular computer systems. These smaller networks facilitate some data and resource sharing without the complicated and costly business of joining a bibliographic utility and contracting to meet its obligations. No one yet knows whether or how the national and international networks will evolve in reaction to these developments.

Cataloging in the Surveyed Libraries

Responses from the surveyed libraries indicated that precatalog searching was done often everywhere, although seven academic and five public libraries had eliminated it. Bibliographic networks frequently were mentioned as being searched (as were other union lists), but searches of local catalogs, shelflists, and order files all were mentioned most frequently as the first step in cataloging.

Naturally, the files most often maintained by the catalog departments of the surveyed libraries were public catalogs, sometimes identified as local computerized systems, and shelflists. In the academic libraries, however, bibliographic

utility files were maintained by twenty-one catalog departments, and local computer network files by eleven. Only five
academic libraries reported having an official catalog in addition to their public catalog. In the public libraries, bibliographic utility files were maintained by twelve catalog departments, and local computer network files by ten. Eight
public libraries reported having an official catalog in addition
to their public catalog. One public librarian said they contributed to a non-computerized union list.

Only five academic libraries reported dividing their cataloging unit into subunits, and serials cataloging was the most
frequently designated subunit. One library had six subunits,
including pre-cataloging, shelflisting, descriptive cataloging,
copy cataloging, data entry, and serials; one had seven units,
including separate subunits for shelflisting, descriptive cataloging, subject cataloging, classification, data entry, copy
cataloging, and serials cataloging; while the others had three
or fewer subunits. Among the public libraries, only four
reported dividing the cataloging unit into subunits. Two of
these indicated shelflisting was the subunit; one reported
having pre-cataloging, data entry, and retrospective conversion subunits; and the fourth reported having subunits for
shelflisting, classification, data entry, and serials cataloging.

Staffing of cataloging units in all the responding libraries
was largely by non-degreed personnel, with at most one or
two degreed librarians serving in the unit. Only two academic
and four public libraries reported employing more than two
degreed professionals in the cataloging unit.

Comments from the responding libraries related primarily
to computer-based systems and operations, including the
following:

"Head of Catalog Section is also NOTIS Project Director . . ."
"Catalog on OCLC with TPS interface to CLSI online catalog."
"Original cataloging performed by paraprofessional; well-
trained technicians handle all but the most difficult copy cataloging tasks."

"Two staff members work full-time . . . librarian = cataloger plus OCLC Coordinator = technician."

"Member copy cataloging performed by high level clerical staff."

"Once the correct record has been identified/verified by the dept. head most of the OCLC input is performed by work-study students. The Dept. Head does original cataloging for the most part only."

Other comments evidenced unusual staffing or operational patterns:

"Volunteers are used extensively in the cataloging unit. I have one volunteer who files all the cards, in both the public catalog and the shelf list. The Public Services Librarian checks the filing in the public catalog and I check the filing in the shelf list . . ."

"Most of our cataloging is done by county system service center. The small amount of original cataloging is done by part time librarian in Technical Services plus reference librarian in Information Services Division."

Conclusion

As the twentieth century draws to a close, a delicate equilibrium exists between local library operations and national and international networks, based on a variety of strategic links. The entity known as the U.S. "national network" is, in reality, a fanciful name for a multiplicity of large and small networks, from OCLC to the tiniest public library microcomputer-based OPAC. Some of the units are linked with one another; others have no direct tie-ins to any other library or computer system. Taken together, they represent a powerful source of information about information—an appropriate concept for the Information Age.

Suggestions for Additional Reading

Burger, Robert H. *Authority Work: The Creation, Use, Maintenance, and Evaluation of Authority Records and Files.* Littleton, CO: Libraries Unlimited, 1985.

Cochrane, Pauline A. *Redesign of Catalogs and Indexes for Improved Online Subject Access*. Phoenix: Oryx Press, 1985.

Crawford, Walt. *Bibliographic Displays in the Online Catalog*. White Plains, NY: Knowledge Industry Publications; Boston: distributed by G.K. Hall, 1986.

───. *Patron Access: Issues for Online Catalogs*. Boston: G.K. Hall, 1987.

Foster, Donald L. *Managing the Catalog Department*, 2nd ed. Metuchen, NJ: Scarecrow Press, 1982.

Hyman, Richard Joseph. *Shelf Access in Libraries*. Chicago: American Library Association, 1982.

Intner, Sheila S. and Richard P. Smiraglia. *Policy and Practice in Bibliographic Control of Nonbook Media*. Chicago: American Library Association, 1987.

Intner, Sheila S. and Jean Weihs. *Standard Cataloging for School and Public Libraries*. Englewood, CO: Libraries Unlimited, 1990.

Mandel, Carol. "Trade-offs: Quantifying Quality in Technical Services," *Journal of Academic Librarianship* 14 (Sept. 1988):214–20.

Martin, Susan K. *Library Networks*, 3rd ed. White Plains, NY: Knowledge Industry Publications; Boston: distributed by G.K. Hall, 1986.

Miksa, Francis. "Cataloging Education in the Library and Information Science Curriculum," in *Recruiting, Educating, and Training Cataloging Librarians*, 273–97.

—6—

Document Delivery Services: Circulation and Interlibrary Loans

Libraries traditionally have delivered documents (i.e., books, films, maps, and all the other types of library materials generically called "documents") to clients through their collections, i.e., by acquiring them, organizing them, storing them, and then devising rules for their use. If the library did not have something one wanted, one could request that it be obtained and in time it might be. Meanwhile, one could buy the wanted item, try another library, or do without it.

Libraries often did not permit their materials to be taken out of buildings, and hours of public service were short. The privilege of using material was not identical for all clients, nor were all materials eligible for identical uses. Many of these traditions remain with us today, embodied in a complicated web of rules for borrowing materials, called "circulation services."

Over the years, however, libraries began to deliver documents in one of two ways: the traditional way, i.e., acquiring and circulating them; or obtaining them temporarily from other sources, usually from other libraries who joined together in cooperative groups in order to share their materials. These temporary acquisitions became known as interlibrary loans, because the shared material was not lent by the owning library directly to the borrower, but to the borrower's library.

The transaction was one between libraries, not between library and client, and rules were devised to govern these, also.

The two kinds of document delivery systems—circulation of a library's own stock and interlibrary loans, or the temporary use of other libraries' stock—have coexisted for quite some time. The proportion of material use resulting from interlibrary loans is small, but ever-present. Generally speaking, if one's library does not own a desired item and cannot obtain it from its interlibrary loan partners, one may be out of luck unless able to buy it personally.

Until the advent of computer-based networks, that was all there was to document delivery services. But along with the new capabilities and services that computer-based systems could accomplish in the areas of acquisitions and cataloging have come new opportunities for service in document delivery. Computers were applied to circulation and interlibrary loans, and enhanced both of them. In addition, they are changing the meaning of document delivery as electronic services alter capabilities and expectations.

New Meaning for Document Delivery

Expansion of document delivery beyond owned materials, i.e., circulation and interlibrary loans, has its roots in other developments not directly involved with delivering library materials. It grew out of efforts to extend bibliographic control over the world's outpouring of published material. The first step in obtaining any document is knowing that it exists, so systems of bibliographic control supply the information that fuel delivery systems.

One contribution to the expansion of document delivery services was standardization of descriptive cataloging so that it could be shared widely, even among different nations of the world. The goal of a universal union catalog was spearheaded by Dorothy Anderson and the cataloging experts who met in Paris and Copenhagen during the 1960s to hammer out the principles on which ISBD and AACR are based.[1] Anderson's Universal Bibliographic Control program set the stage for bibliographic data sharing on a grand scale. Less than a decade later, Henriette Avram's design of the MARC communications format for machine-readable data at LC and Frederick Kilgour's plans for the OCLC network inaugurated the implementation of the first large-scale national (and later international) computer-based data sharing project.

Another contribution to expanding the definition of document delivery beyond owned materials was application of computers to the publishing process, especially for preparation of periodical indexes. Subsequently, the publishers began to experiment with distribution of their machine-readable databases directly to consumers via computer. These developments led to the rise of information brokers such as Lockheed's DIALOG, Bibliographic Retrieval Services, and the Systems Development Corporation's ORBIT service, which distributed not one but many databases through telecommunications networks that linked consumers with the broker. So far, this process parallels the first development, being a compilation and distribution of bibliographic citations, except that the body of literature being represented is not books and other library materials, but periodical articles, research reports, book chapters, etc.

One of the information brokers' services to their industrial and major governmental customers was document delivery, providing them with the full texts of the documents represented in database citations. At first, brokers gave searchers with the appropriate charge accounts the option of requesting offprints of cited articles with a few keystrokes. The offprints were mailed to the requester within twenty-four hours. Later, they also began to supply the full text of some articles immediately by displaying them on the terminals. Soon, customers discovered that if they had the correct equipment and software, they could capture both bibliographic data and text by downloading it onto a disk or tape into their local system. Here was a new form of document delivery, indeed.

The combination of these two developments has resulted in a broadening of the definition of document delivery, and the rise of a new dichotomy in librarianship, namely, that of access versus ownership.

BROADENING THE DEFINITION OF DOCUMENT DELIVERY

The evolution of international cataloging networks (such as OCLC) and reference networks (such as DIALOG) began similarly, although the two types of networks addressed different bodies of literature. OCLC and its companions dealt primarily with information about library materials, mostly books, while DIALOG and its companions dealt primarily with information about periodical articles, research reports, and other items too small to be given separate catalog records by libraries. Libraries were enthusiastic subscribers to DIALOG and the other database brokers, although, unlike corporate users, few nonprofit libraries took advantage of the document supply services. Instead, libraries tended to continue to rely on whatever periodical titles they owned, plus the option of interlibrary loans for the rest. Pressure from clients to purchase more periodical titles increased, however, and larger shares of library budgets began being allocated to journal subscriptions.

Delivery of full text as well as bibliographic data is something the OCLC group also has the technology to accomplish; but because the size of individual documents is much larger and because the networks do not own the rights to reproduce and sell them, they have not attempted to implement document delivery services.

Toward the end of the 1980s, a new category of player began to emerge in what was becoming known as the electronic marketplace: publishers of electronic texts. Distribution of indexes in electronic form is not very difficult and much less costly than distribution of the printed versions, once the equipment and communications software is in place. Now, some indexes are being published *solely* in electronic format, as are some journal titles, encyclopedias and other reference tools, and governmental data. The number of electronically published titles is small, but growing, and it can only be expected to increase in the future.

In the 1960s, a number of library experts predicted a scenario in which electronically-delivered information became the principal data source for information seekers, calling it the "paperless society."[2] Ten years afterward, when the production of paper-and-print publications was still increasing, librarians thought it was all a mistake; but they neglected to realize it would take some time until all the pieces were in place, and that the rise of the new format would not replace the old one entirely. As the final decade of the century progresses, things seem to be moving in the direction foreseen by the library experts thirty years earlier—and by other visionaries twenty years before that.[3]

The literature of scholarly communication in general, and that of humanities and social sciences disciplines in particular, now is filled with articles about electronic publishing and its implications. One of the characteristics of electronic text is the ease with which it can be requested, used, and erased, which has led librarians to wonder whether permanent acquisition and storage of materials may become less and less important. Further, the ease with which electronic text can be altered has led scholars and librarians alike to wonder whether a proliferation of multiple iterations of a text, each with changes from the others, may replace traditional notions of the immutability of individually published texts.

A growing number of scholars have exchanged their pre-computer invisible college (i.e., personal network of scholarly contacts) operating sporadically by letter, telephone, and person-to-person meetings at conferences, for a new, computer-based collegial telecommunications network that operates around the clock at little cost and with few limitations. Beginning with researchers in the hard sciences, for whom the computer's processing of large amounts of statistical data was a key to great new breakthroughs, interest in and attachment to computing has spread to all disciplines, mainly via the attraction of word processing. Once one learns to use a computer for one thing, it is not very difficult to use it for others, particularly since software developers are aware of the enormous market potential for easy-to-use software.

As scholarly computing and electronic publishing are now

realities, so is the notion that libraries need not acquire and store all needed materials if they can ensure that whenever something is needed, it can be called up on the library's or the scholar's computer screen. This kind of document delivery service still is in its infancy, but given the speed with which the technology has developed and the power of its scope, librarians might expect that it soon will begin to define document delivery services, not merely enhance them.

ACCESS VERSUS OWNERSHIP

Since the rise of scholarly computing, there has been a tug of war between computer-based materials and ordinary printed ones. In some colleges and universities, computer-based information services are not located in the library, but in computer centers, where they are controlled by data processing administrators, not librarians. In a few institutions, the situation is reversed and the library is the focus of all academic computing activity, along with all other ordinary academic information resources.[4] What is important is that in most places, clear distinctions are made between the information obtained through computerized sources and that available from library-owned materials, even when they are all administered by the library.

The computer-based information system is perceived by librarians as affording "access" but not ownership of the information it contains, whether bibliographic citations or full texts, since all the library acquires is the right to access it. While the library user might copy and store some of the data from the computer-based service, it is assumed (or contractually required) that the library will not copy the entire database and store it indefinitely on its premises. Access is contrasted with the ownership of materials—mostly printed materials—whose physical presence in the library is acquired along with the right to use them.

The dichotomy between access and ownership of materials is a troubling issue that has engaged more than one expert.[5] It portends to become the major issue of the 1990s and beyond, affecting trends in collection development, organization of materials, and document delivery.

Circulating Materials

Although the foregoing sections serve to highlight the changing nature of library document delivery, for the immediate future, use of library materials undoubtedly will remain a function of circulation services. These are the services that govern borrowing library materials for varying lengths of time by members of the library's user population. Borrowing materials is the most visible service that libraries provide to the public, and even in-house use of reference materials often is called internal or in-house "circulation." An understanding of circulation is important, since it is a critical link between library materials and the people for whom they are intended.

Elements of the circulation function. A circulation system has three elements: borrowers, materials, and transactions. The most obvious purpose of the circulation system is to keep track of these three elements, particularly the library's materials, but there are other important circulation objectives also. These include facilitating the use of materials, knowing what materials are being used, how frequently they are being used, and by whom. To maintain complete control over circulation, all three elements need to be tracked comprehensively. At the same time, the circulation system must include a means of indicating to borrowers when materials are due. Ideally, librarians would want lists of all potential borrowers, all borrowable materials, and all borrowing transactions, as well as an efficient way to provide needed information for the borrowers; however, not every circulation system furnishes the same kinds of information, the same degree of control, or the same level of information feedback to the librarians monitoring it.

One of the simplest methods of keeping track of borrowed materials is to record the transactions somewhere in the library so that the librarian can determine whom to contact if materials are not returned. One can write the names of the borrowers and the materials in a ledger that has a page for each borrower, or a page (or more) for each day, thus maintaining a circulation file arranged either by borrower or in chronological order. The problem with ledgers is that neither arrangement affords easy retrieval of all the information librarians might need, and they are not easy to use. When something is returned, for example, the librarian has to find the page where the transaction was recorded and cancel it or otherwise indicate the material was returned. This method is not unlike keeping a book catalog or an accession list, and it is not used much anymore.

Another method of recording transactions is to provide each transaction with a form, or slip, (called a "t-slip") with spaces for the item's bibliographic information, the name of the borrower, and the date. When an item is borrowed, the slip is filled out and filed in the library. One could arrange a file of such slips in any number of ways—by call number, by title or main entry, by date borrowed or date due, or even by the borrower's name. Until the advent of computing, this was a very popular method of keeping track of circulation information.

A similar method, also very popular, is to issue a card with bibliographic information on it for each borrowable item. When the item is borrowed, the borrower signs his or her name on the card, which remains in the library, along with the date the item is due. This saves the client from having to write out the bibliographic information for the item. Item cards (or, "book cards" as they are known even when they are used for films, sound recordings, or other nonbook materials) and t-slips can be employed singly or in multiple copies, depending on the library's information needs. Libraries that want to recall borrowed items before their due dates (frequently desired in academic settings) may keep two files— one arranged by due date (so overdues can be found easily) and one arranged by call number, title, or main entry (for recalls). Multiple files tend to be more popular in academic than in public library settings.

Both card and transaction slip circulation systems usually place a pocket in the borrowable items, to hold the book card(s), t-slip(s), and/or the separately processed due date card or slip. Book cards and pockets are available from library suppliers, and a number of software products have been designed to produce imprinted cards and pockets or card and pocket labels automatically for any item cataloged. There are several variations on the card theme. One variant is to issue patron cards bearing numbered metal plates that stamp the borrower's unique card number and a due date on the book card when something is borrowed. Library suppliers sell the machinery and the cards, and they have become popular because they provide a more legible record while simultaneously saving clients the tedium of signing their names. The library card also serves to identify eligible borrowers quickly and easily to circulation staff members, and the automatic stamping machine helps to speed up the checkout process. The stamping machines have to be set with the proper dates and filled with ink every day, and although they are reliable, they jam occasionally and require regular cleaning and maintenance.

A second variant based on book cards and patron identification cards (i.e., library cards) employs a camera that takes a microphotograph of the book card, a numbered transaction card imprinted with a due date, and the borrower's library card together. The library retains the microfilm record, and the client retains all the cards with the item. Sometimes there is no book card per se, just a pocket labelled with the bibliographic data that is matched with the transaction card and the library card for the microphotograph. The borrower does not have to write anything, the library gets a legible record, albeit on microfilm, and the checkout transaction is quick and easy. The cameras have to be loaded with film and maintained, but they tend to be reliable machines that do not break down very often.

Computerized circulation systems employ machine-readable labels of various kinds to identify materials, borrowers, and transactions, coupled with databases that provide full bibliographic, personal, and loan information. One popular type of identification label is the bar code, called a "zebra" label because of the black and white stripes. When the zebra label is read into the computer, either by a scanning device or by keying it in, the record(s) it represents are retrieved from storage and displayed on the terminal. Another popular label is the optical character recognition label (OCR), which represents the relevant data in a font that can be read by a person or a computer. Human operators must record transactions by entering data for the borrower and the borrowed material into the system. Depending on the type of software, the computer might do the rest automatically, updating all its files as each piece of data is fed into the system, tracking overdues and fees, producing reports and notices, deleting open transactions when materials are returned, and even beeping borrowers who have exceeded the library's preset borrowing limits. Or, the human operators might receive coded data produced by the computer which they have to translate or manipulate further in order to print notices, reports, etc. Recording due dates in borrowed materials might or might not be part of the work done by the computer system. Many librarians continue to use manually-prepared due date cards, slips, or date stamps, because their computer systems were not programmed to produce separate due date records automatically.

Summing up, circulation systems must have methods of identifying eligible borrowers and materials, recording the borrowing transactions, and giving the borrowers notice of the due date. Borrowers might be issued special library cards, or they might substitute academic identification cards, driver's licenses, or other types of identification instead. Materials might be given identifying book cards and/or appropriately labelled pockets, or the burden of recording the bibliographic information might rest with the borrower. Computer systems might employ bar codes or OCR labels for borrower and material identification. Transactions recorded on one or more slips, cards, or microfilm, or in the case of computer systems, in a database of transactions, are retained by the library for use in the event the materials are not returned in a timely fashion.

The application of computers to circulation data gave libraries the opportunity to combine the three types of circulation data into an integrated database system having many important new capabilities. The computer-based system provides greater control over the whereabouts of library materials as well as automatic filing and updating of circulation information when new data is fed into the system. When a borrowed item is returned, for example, providing this information to the computer by means of a check-in scan of the item label will not only cancel the transaction, but update the item's location data, the patron's outstanding holdings data, etc.

CIRCULATION CONTROL VERSUS TRACKING OVERDUES

At the very least, circulation systems must keep track of materials that become overdue so they can be recalled. Some circulation systems really do nothing more than this, e.g., although the microfilmed circulation data in the system described above includes identification of materials and borrowers as well as borrowing transactions, it would be very hard to find out whether a wanted item was borrowed, or who borrowed a wanted item, without examining all the transactions on all the rolls of microfilm one by one until the right one was found. The transactions on the microfilm are arranged in the order the pictures are taken, and that is the only way they can be searched. The data is used solely to find transactions that have not been cancelled (i.e., transactions for which cards are not returned or for which picture numbers have not been checked off) before perusal of a particular day's or week's microfilms. Any transactions still outstanding will be located by picture number on the microfilm so that notices that the items are past due can be typed and sent to the borrowers.

All single slip or card systems arranged chronologically work this way and are used primarily to track overdues. These files can be and often are searched for borrower or material data, but it is a difficult task. Searching is easier if eye-readable slips or cards in the daily files are sub-arranged alphabetically by title or main entry or by call number. They are much easier to search manually than microfilms, since the microphotographs cannot be rearranged.

Multiple slip or card systems provide easier access to data for materials and/or patrons, and are preferred in libraries that want easy access to borrower or material data before due dates have been breached. Nevertheless, even they keep track solely of materials that have been borrowed. They do not keep records of items that are not borrowed, but assume all materials that have not been borrowed are where they belong on the shelves.

Circulation control systems go beyond tracking borrowed materials, and maintain files for all of the library's borrowable materials whether or not they are on loan, and all of the library's borrowers, whether or not they have anything checked out at the moment, as well as all the borrowing transactions. It is an inventory and customer control system in which borrowable items comprise the inventory and borrowers are the customers. Part of the system is a reporting function that can furnish important information about the use of materials to librarians. Inventory records can be tracked to see how frequently items are used as well as whether they are on loan or waiting to be borrowed; customer records can be tracked to see whether borrowers owe any money to the library and what items they currently have on loan.

Computerized circulation control systems are so good at tracking past activity in the system they must be programmed to erase previous borrowing records to preserve borrowers' personal privacy. Generally, once a transaction ends, all the library wishes to retain in its records are fees owed, if any. It may be useful for collection developers to find out the subject areas in which library borrowers are interested, but a fine line must be observed between obtaining this information with the individuals' consent and gathering it without their knowledge. For this reason, activity of materials in various subject areas is tracked from the materials' item records, not from the borrowers' records.

POLICIES AND PRACTICES

Circulation is one of the few library functions that has a long tradition of written policies, probably because they are necessary to avoid having constantly to explain the rules of borrowing to clients. The rules of circulation, i.e., circulation policies, state *who* may borrow materials, *what* materials will be lent and for *how long*, and *what will happen* when someone does not return borrowed materials on time.[6]

Each element has many decisions associated with it. Regarding borrowers, a library will decide first who are their primary constituents based on residence, enrollment, etc., and then they will distinguish among different types of borrowers based on factors such as age, educational level, etc. Subsequently, they will make decisions about other persons who can be served even though they are not part of the primary constituency, along with any special exceptions or inclusions.

Nothing is simple in the decision making for each element, unless an effort is made deliberately to perceive it that way. Even very small public libraries may have ten or more different categories of borrowers, including adult, young adult, and child residents, temporary residents, employees of residents, adult nonresident taxpayers and their dependents or employees, nonresident students and faculty attending or teaching in community schools, fee-paying nonresidents, and residents of communities with which the library has a contractual or information cooperative borrowing agreement. Similar kinds of complications can apply to materials, and ten or more types of different loans that vary further by type of borrower are not uncommon, unless library decision-makers choose to ignore the differences and treat all (or virtually all) materials alike for borrowing purposes.

Libraries also must make decisions about what they will do when materials are not returned by the designated due date. Some libraries feel obliged to send one or more notices to borrowers, reminding them that their materials are overdue. Lately, however, library policies have begun to express the belief that such reminders are a courtesy, not an obligation, and that borrowers are fully responsible for materials and penalties for late returns whether or not the library reminds them. Typically, a schedule of penalties—small fines and fees—for overdue items is imposed, often with limits of a few dollars on their maximum accumulation. Critics argue that the charges are too low to have any impact on the prompt return of materials. Fines may be tied both to the types of materials and the categories of borrowers as well as to the type of transaction (e.g., a one-week loan or a four-week loan). Multiplying the potential number of material categories by the potential number of borrowing categories, and that result by the number of transaction types, it is easy to see how hundreds of different fine categories might result.

Several trends in circulation policies have been observed in the last decade, during which many libraries computerized their circulation operations:

1. Public librarians seemed to be broadening their vision of who should be eligible to borrow materials from concentrating solely on local constituencies to including state-wide and regional constituencies.
2. Some larger academic libraries seemed to be narrowing their view of who should be eligible to borrow materials from a perception that any scholar or member of their local communities should be welcome to concentrating solely on their own institutional constituencies.
3. "Stack" books (i.e., older, non-reference books) were the primary circulating materials, while new books, periodicals, and other nonbook materials were likely to have restrictions on being borrowed.
4. Daily fine charges remained very low, while lost book charges were increasing rapidly to meet to actual cost of replacement plus processing.
5. Computer-based systems were not being used to send more notices, but to supply more up-to-date information about clients and material use.
6. Withdrawal of borrowing privileges as a penalty was being imposed more frequently, especially in libraries where computer-based systems enabled librarians to identify borrowers who consistently contravened the rules.

What seems to be most important for successful circulation policies is to have clearly defined objectives and a cohesive set of procedures that satisfy them. Computerizing the operation is not enough to make it succeed; the way the computer-based system is used is much more important. Librarians using computer-based circulation systems want them to be integrated with computer-based cataloging, acquisitions, and reference systems. They seem less ambitious about providing new services than handling traditional borrowing more effectively.

Interlibrary Loans

Another way libraries provide materials to their clients is by borrowing them from other libraries. This service, called interlibrary loan (ILL), has a long history, but generally has not accounted for large proportions of delivered documents. Traditionally, ILL has been lauded more in theory than in practice. In practice, ILL could take many days or weeks, and by the time an item arrived, the borrower might have lost interest or decided to do without it. ILL can involve costly procedures that libraries prefer to avoid, so they may choose not to publicize the service, place limits on the borrowers who can be served, charge fees for the service, or otherwise discourage its use.

In many places, clients must make special requests for ILL, and sometimes only one staff member is designated to accept them. Clients may be required to fill out lengthy forms, and the forms might be put into a queue until they are verified by another staff member. Only after verification will the request be sent out to other libraries. Requests used to be sent by mail and still are in many libraries, which takes additional time. And it is not just the requesting library's procedures that might impede speedy ILL service. When the request arrives at the receiving library, it might have to wait for attention from a particular staff member, or the material might not be available, or it might turn out to be designated a non-ILL item. Several days might elapse before the negative message is sent, once again by mail, received by the requesting library, and transmitted to the waiting borrower. Since the most critical factor for ILL service from the borrower's point of view is waiting time, procedures such as these that add to its length tend to bar use of ILL by any but the most determined and patient information seekers.

Despite all the potential barriers to its success, ILL has remained part of most libraries' stated document delivery services. Then, in the 1970s, the advent of computerized bibliographic networks suddenly provided new opportunities for faster ILL service. In the sections that follow, ILL methods and the changes brought about by computerization are discussed, as well as the resulting implications for collection management.

METHODS OF LENDING BETWEEN LIBRARIES

Efforts to codify ILL procedures have been made over the years by librarians working in their local and state library organizations, the American Library Association, and elsewhere. Model codes were drawn up to assist groups of libraries wishing to cooperate on ILL in designing a workable set of rules that apportioned responsibilities fairly between the libraries making ILL requests and those receiving and filling them. The model group code and a model national-level code described below,[7] were developed by a committee of the American Library Association's Reference and Adult Services Division and published in 1981. The national code is intended for use by libraries that are acting individually, outside of any group, and have no other rules to follow. Neither code is binding on any institution or group of institutions, but they have had substantial influence over current practices.[8]

The need for a fair apportionment of responsibilities is clear, since ILL borrowing and lending rarely is identical for any institution. Libraries with large, rich collections usually receive more requests than they make to smaller partners. This puts them in the sometimes uncomfortable position of being "net lenders" (i.e., on balance, lending more than they borrow) to their partners.[9] If the costs and/or obligations of ILL transactions fall more heavily on the lenders than the borrowers, net lenders might begin to wonder whether participating in the partnership is worthwhile, since not only do they lend more materials than they receive, but it costs them more to do it. Furthermore, the wear and tear on ILL-borrowed materials could be considerably greater than on locally borrowed materials, aggravating the issue. Thus, provisions of model codes attempt to strike a balance that minimizes the burdens on lenders and defines appropriate and inappropriate requests. Some states that wish to encourage their statewide ILL networks may choose to reimburse libraries for ILL transactions. When this is the case, net lenders earn something for their efforts.

The model code for groups of libraries is written to accommodate options, e.g., the scope statement says:

> Under the terms of this agreement, it is permissible to request on interlibrary loan any type of library material [except . . .][10]

This allows any group of libraries using the model to exclude categories of materials from ILL without extensive rewriting. The secondary, or supplemental nature of ILL (compared with owning and circulating a library's own materials) is an underlying assumption of the code, which states clearly that ILL is not a substitute for buying the materials needed by one's clients.[11] The responsibilities of borrowing libraries, in addition to buying needed materials, include using ILL codes and standard procedures, educating staff and clients, complying with copyright law, supplying full identifying data in the request, guarding the safety of ILLs, and complying with the lender's rules. The requesting library also is supposed to encourage its clients to go to the owning library in person to obtain desired material, thus eliminating ILL requests if possible.[12] The list of responsibilities of the lending library first absolves it from lending anything it does not wish to share, and then requires that it publicize its ILL policies, process requests promptly, and report failure to fill requests.[13] The lending library should not count time spent in transit in its loan period, and it is permitted to charge fees for its material, although if the fee is "more than nominal," it must ascertain that the borrowing library has authorized payment.[14]

The national code differs in some respects, although it, too, declares that ILL should not replace collection development.

Unlike the group code, which places no limits on the purposes of ILL, the national code assumes that ILL will not be used frivolously, stating, "The purpose of interlibrary loan as defined in this code is to obtain, for research and serious study, library material not available through local, state, or regional libraries."[15] The code names the types of materials that usually are excluded, including rare, valuable, bulky, fragile, high-demand, and/or unique materials, and materials subject to local circulation restrictions.[16] In the balance of the code, the responsibilities of borrowing and lending libraries are spelled out. While these are virtually the same as in the group code, there are some notable differences, e.g., borrowers are told to "avoid concentrating the burden of requests on a few libraries";[17] and the final provision relating to violations of the rules is worded punitively, unlike the group code, which puts each partner on its honor to fulfill its obligations.[18]

Both model codes clarify the subordinate role in document delivery to be played by ILL. Libraries are urged to buy what they need for repeated use, and it is assumed that ILL will not be used to obtain materials the need for which could have been anticipated in advance. The elimination from ILL of high-demand materials absolves libraries from guilt over refusing to lend an item thought to be needed by their own clients.

IMPACT OF THE BIBLIOGRAPHIC UTILITIES

Before the rise of the computerized bibliographic networks, ILL service was slow and finding out who held a particular document was no simple task. ILL was unlikely to be used casually to satisfy a client's passing fancy to have a look at something, and libraries were not supposed to think of ILL as an alternative to purchase. But in the latter half of the 1970s and the beginning of the 1980s, it became clear that libraries could not buy everything they needed. The information explosion not only continued, but intensified, and the value of acquisition dollars steadily diminished. At the same time, the strength and size of the bibliographic networks were growing, and one of their primary objectives was to promote resource sharing among their members. The development of huge databases of bibliographic information with the electronic linkages needed for instantaneous transmission of ILL requests contributed to a sudden surge of ILL that startled the library community and even caused some publishers to tremble.

The principle of the ILL cooperative—sharing materials among partners—was the same as it had always been, but the scale had changed. In OCLC, instead of handfuls of partners, there were hundreds of member libraries that quickly grew into thousands. Instead of union lists containing a few hundred thousand titles, the Online Union Catalog contained records for millions of titles, and each record included a list of holding libraries that could be called up with just four or five simple keystrokes. In place of weeks of waiting time, ILL turnarounds began to be measured in days and later, in some favored places, in hours. As the 1980s progressed, the number of OCLC ILL transactions began to be measured in six figures, with shorter lapses of time between each succeeding million. In RLIN, which had fewer than fifty members, the sizes of the collections being shared were so large and their contents so diverse that even this smaller network rapidly became an ILL resource of truly gigantic proportions.

Three attributes of computerized bibliographic networks turned ILL into an important source of needed materials:

1. The size and diversity of network databases, measured in millions of records representing all kinds of materials;
2. The ability of the records to include and display lists of holding libraries;
3. The telecommunications links among participating libraries that permitted electronic messages to be sent virtually instantaneously from any member to any other member or group of members.

Library computing revolutionized ILL, bringing it to prominence at just the time libraries were starving for acquisition dollars.

INTERLIBRARY LOANS AND COLLECTION MANAGEMENT

The more critical the collection development outlook became in terms of the amount of materials available for purchase against the dollars available for acquisitions in the fifteen year period between 1975 and 1990, the more effective and efficient the national bibliographic networks were becoming in their support for ILL. Libraries made up of multiple units and cooperative groups began to retrench. They started to assess the degree of duplication of resources among their constituents to determine whether overlaps could be eliminated and total resources available through intra- and/or interlibrary loans maximized. For the first time, outside of a nucleus of high-demand materials that each library had to purchase to make available immediately on request, librarians began to look beyond their own collections for materials they knew would be needed in the future, and make commitments to share larger proportions of their holdings.

The size of regional and local networks continues to grow and their computing power continues to increase. Although no one talks openly about making such decisions, clearly the stage is set for each individual library in a group to buy titles its partners need but will not buy, planning instead to interloan them for their clients. Publishers have warned that these decisions can have disastrous effects on the production of low-demand materials, such as the highly specialized scholarly works collected by research libraries. They believe increased ILL will mean that a small scholarly press will be able to sell only a few dozen copies of a title instead of hundreds or thousands of copies. Coupled with the continued absorption of independent publishing houses by profit-oriented conglomerates that will not tolerate low-profit titles, industry experts predict a dire future for the production of scholarly information.

No matter what the outcome, librarians are re-evaluating the place of ILL in their collection development plans. The issue of ownership versus access is not merely one of subscriptions to computerized databases, but also one of purchase versus ILL.

Other Access Systems

ELECTRONIC DELIVERY OF INFORMATION

A great deal is being written about computer-based information systems that do more than provide information about
documents, i.e., systems that furnish the documents themselves on request. This kind of electronic delivery of information is spreading in business and industry, but it does not
appear to be ubiquitous yet. Probably because of its cost, it is
appearing even more slowly in libraries. Three types of electronic full text products are being marketed to libraries:

1. Online indexes of bibliographic citations that include full
   texts for all or some of the materials;
2. Journals, encyclopedias, and other works issued originally
   as computer-based products;
3. Electronic bulletin boards, i.e., electronically transmitted
   public communication systems that facilitate the exchange of contributions from all persons using the system.

Online indexes have been discussed above. They deal most
frequently with citations for journal articles, some of which
can be reproduced in full should the library choose to pay for
the service. The likelihood that longer works such as monographic books might be distributed this way is not discussed
much, partly because of the length of time and cost in paper,
printer ribbons, and equipment wear and tear it would take
to print whole books, and partly because permission to reproduce books on demand is difficult to obtain. Products that
successfully reproduce sounds and visual images through
computer terminals are still in the experimental stages and
are quite costly, so very little literature discusses computer-
based access to lengthy sound and visual works such as
symphonies, films, etc. Nevertheless, there is no *technological*
reason why whole books could not be transmitted to libraries
by computer and printed on demand by a client at a terminal
attached to a printer.

Electronic journals, electronic encyclopedias, electronic
Bibles, etc., are becoming more popular as library materials,

although they still are something of a novelty. The growing use by libraries of computer-based indexes on CD-ROM disks, which requires that library computers be fitted with CD-ROM disk drives, has led producers to introduce more works on CD-ROM that can be used on the same equipment. CD-ROM storage is an attractive medium for works comprising large amounts of text that change continuously over time, albeit slowly, for several reasons:

1. It is much less costly to provide text on disk than via continuous online access;
2. A small, reliable, virtually indestructible disk is able to hold large amounts of text in digitized form;
3. The library receives a disk as tangible evidence they are purchasing something;
4. The producer can update the source database continuously and issue new versions on disk frequently, holding onto purchasers of the initial products by keeping them well satisfied.

Reference tools such as catalogs and directories, indexes, encyclopedias, almanacs, etc. are one category of library material that does well in the CD-ROM medium. Another category is made up of large works (such as Bibles) that include dynamic auxiliary writings such as commentaries or literary criticism. A third category consists of multimedia packages of videorecordings and computer software such as the pioneering Emperor I project of Ching-chih Chen.[19] Although still in the experimental stages, video- and computer-based multimedia systems (sometimes termed "hypermedia") may provide the most exciting new access to information ever imagined by giving each user the opportunity to interact with the material uniquely to create an individualized information package.

Electronic bulletin boards are the last of the newer computer-based access media considered in this chapter. An electronic bulletin board, or "bboard" is a computer-based open message system designed to allow its users opportunities to exchange information. Bboard services on a national and international scale are offered both by commercial and scholarly networks. Local bboard services abound, catering to all sorts of interest areas and groups of people, e.g., in companies, clubs, professional organizations, academic institutions, etc. Who can say that the transmission of an article on a bboard is not the same as its publication in a journal? Thus, bboards afford a new kind of document delivery service for materials that could be unavailable anywhere else.

IMPACT ON TECHNICAL SERVICES

The impact of the newest types of computer-based document delivery services on technical services has not reached revolutionary proportions yet, primarily because few libraries are implementing them on a large scale for masses of users. However, one of the key features of electronically transmitted documents is that they may not require specific acquisition, cataloging, or processing, and that "circulation" or use is part of a larger set of services bundled into a network package. Library technical services might be bypassed completely, or if not, might be ineffectual in organizing works lacking physical manifestations whose acquisition, organization, and use must be controlled by the library.

Document Delivery in the Surveyed Libraries

Technical services departments of the surveyed libraries have administrative authority over circulation services in only four libraries, and all are public libraries. Sixteen more libraries, both academic and public, indicated that authority over circulation services is held by an "administrative services unit," often the same unit to which the technical services department reports. In these libraries, circulation and technical services are perceived as separate but related departments at the same level of organizational hierarchy, and belonging together in the same unit. In contrast, twenty-eight of the surveyed libraries placed circulation services under the authority of the public services unit. This would indicate that circulation is perceived by a larger number of libraries in terms of its interactions with the public (i.e., stamping out books, receiving returned books, requesting and collecting fees and fines) than in terms of its technical inventory control and maintenance aspects (i.e., shelving, collection maintenance, and record keeping).

Most, but not all, of the surveyed libraries maintained four circulation files, i.e., for patrons, transactions, holds, and overdues/fines. The differences between public and academic library responses seemed to demonstrate that public libraries expend more effort on circulation files than do their academic counterparts. For example, only eleven of the academic libraries claimed to maintain hold files, but twenty of the public libraries do. Thirteen of the academic libraries maintain patron files, while nineteen of the public libraries do. Sixteen of the academic libraries maintain overdue/fine files, but twenty of the public libraries do.

Staffing of the circulation unit was divided, with fewer than half of each type of library group reporting having one librarian, full- or half-time, assigned to the unit. In most libraries, both public and academic, the number of clerical staff members was larger than the number of paraprofessional staff members. On the other hand, there were far fewer assistants/pages working in the public library circulation departments than in the academic library circulation departments.

Most, but not all, of the surveyed libraries said they supplied statistical reports on circulation activity—seventeen in each type of library group. Six academic and five public libraries furnished financial reports; even fewer reported on transactions, patrons, or any other types of circulation activity.

A few libraries divided their circulation units into subunits, and these indicated that shelving and shelf reading subunits were most often designated, while separate subunits for notice preparation, filing, and desk duties were encountered less frequently.

Conclusion

Circulation services and interlibrary loans remain the chief methods by which libraries furnish materials to patrons. Access to data in computer-based systems does not appear to be a replacement for ownership of materials, and circulation departments are still primarily concerned about charging and discharging materials, preparing overdue and fine notices, and registering patrons. Exciting new computer-based materials that will support electronic delivery of information are developing rapidly, but have yet to be implemented widely. Expanding computer power in libraries, greater computing knowledge on the part of librarians, and more computer-based products from publishers will undoubtedly make inroads into the traditional services of circulation and ILL. The questions that still loom large are how much change lies ahead in the near term and how quickly it will happen.

Suggestions for Additional Reading

CIRCULATION SERVICES

Bernstein, Judith, ed. *Turn-Key Automated Circulation Systems: Aids to Libraries in the Market Place.* Prepared by the Circulation Systems Evaluation Committee, Circulation Services Section, Library Administration and Management Association, American Library Association. Chicago: American Library Association, 1980.

Boss, Richard W. and Judith McQueen. "Automated Circulation Control Systems," *Library Technology Reports* 18 (Mar./Apr. 1982): 3–126.

Burr, Robert I. "Toward a General Theory of Circulation." Urbana: University of Illinois, Graduate School of Library and Information Science, 1977. (Master's thesis).

Fayen, Emily G. "Automated Circulation Systems for Large Libraries." *Library Technology Reports* 22 (July/Aug. 1986): 385–469.

Geer, Helen Thornton. *Charging Systems.* Chicago: American Library Association, 1955.

George Fry & Associates, Inc. *Study of Circulation Control Systems: Public Libraries, College and University Libraries, Special Libraries.* Chicago: Library Technology Project of the American Library Association and the Council on Library Resources, 1961.

Intner, Sheila S. *Circulation Policy in Academic, Public, and School Libraries.* Westport, CT: Greenwood Press, 1987.

INTERLIBRARY LOANS

Boucher, Virginia. *Interlibrary Loan Practices Handbook.* Chicago: American Library Association, 1984.

Cornish, Graham P. *Model Handbook for Interlending and Copying.* Boston Spa: IFLA Office for International Lending and the British Library Document Supply Centre, 1988.

Interlibrary Loan Codes, 1980. American Library Association, Reference and Adult Services Division, Interlibrary Loan Committee, [and] *International Lending Principles and Guidelines, 1978.* International Federation of Library Associations and Institutions, Section on Interlending. Chicago: American Library Association, 1981.

Morris, Leslie, and Patsy Brautigan. *Interlibrary Loan Policies Directory*, 3d ed. New York: Neal-Schuman Publishers, 1988.

—7—

Coordinated
Collection Development

Cooperative projects are not new to libraries, and many existing projects and programs enable one library's constituents to use materials owned by other libraries. One such resource sharing program is interlibrary loan, and another is the extension of borrowing privileges to persons outside a library's own constituency. But sharing the materials a library happens to have is not the same as sharing with other libraries the processes of deciding what materials to buy and purchasing them in concert with the expressed intention of sharing their use among the group's constituencies. This extension of collection development processes from each one of a number of individual libraries to a group effort made by previously independent libraries will be discussed in this chapter under the rubric "coordinated collection development."

The first tentative steps toward coordinated collection development began to be taken in the late 1970s and early 1980s, when the combination of financial exigencies and continuing explosion of information production was juxtaposed against maturing bibliographic networking and growing library computing capabilities. The primary motivating factor behind coordinated collection development undoubtedly was the perceived need for methods of combating libraries' loss of buying power in the face of availability of more purchasable materials. However, the need alone might not have spurred so complex a response without the presence of two other developments: knowledge of sophisticated planning techniques and availability of needed data to underpin planning and implementation. All of these elements came together during the decade of the 1980s, making true coordination of collection development among libraries possible for the first time, in contrast with simply allowing unilaterally developed collections to be shared.

Setting the Stage for
Coordinated Collection Development

The sophisticated planning techniques referred to above are known collectively as strategic planning. Strategic planning, in which long term goals and objectives are identified, agreed upon, and translated into strategies with short term objectives that lead, step by step, toward the larger goals, has been practiced and refined for years by big business and government enterprises. In those settings, the use of strategic planning enabled private companies and governmental agencies to accomplish ambitious undertakings lasting longer than a single fiscal year. Strategic planning made it easier for managers to demonstrate accountability at the end of the plan and to report on their progress during the interim to critical funding groups such as stockholders or legislators.

Strategic planning is a long-term systematic planning effort that operates in much the same way that management by objective, also a systematic planning effort, does for the shorter term. Regardless of the time span involved, systematic planning depends on the organization's commitment to reach a specified set of goals, and to make decisions at operational levels that are consistent with and promote those goals.

All planning and decision making, including strategic planning whether shared or not, need to be supported by the data necessary to set goals, whether long- or short-term, devise operational strategies, and implement them. Most important among the supporting data for collection builders are bibliographic data. Shared bibliographic databases containing millions of entries for current and retrospective materials now are available at local levels as well as at the national level. The advent of regional and local computer networks with sophisticated software enhancements providing access to national databases by individual libraries has made this possible. Needed data can be manipulated and communicated to numerous local recipients simultaneously.

With access to large bibliographic databases, local and regional network members were able to develop databases of information relevant to their particular needs that national networks might find out of scope, such as studies of collection overlaps, or comparisons of holdings by subject, age, etc.[1] Studies of collection distribution, overlap, etc., provide detailed knowledge about the existing holdings of the libraries wishing to coordinate their collecting plans. Obtaining and reviewing this data is an essential part of the process of coordinating collection development.

Comparing the holdings of the several libraries in the group and arriving at mutually held conclusions about them are important elements in making decisions for coordinated collection development. Judging the quality of collections, however, is extremely subjective. The same statistics can be and are interpreted differently by different librarians. For example, if Library A holds 55 percent of the titles in Bibliography X, one librarian might conclude it is enough to call Library A's holdings "excellent," whereas other librarians might conclude they are merely "good," or even "weak." The level of excellence, like beauty, is in the eye of the beholder. Clearly, more objective measures need to be used among groups of libraries wishing to coordinate their collecting, since all the parties must agree about what will be collected and all of them should expect to be equally well satisfied with the results.

Tools of Coordinated Collection Development: The Research Libraries Group *Conspectus*

Members of the Research Libraries Group that founded RLIN were instrumental in developing objective methods of making collection comparisons. It is not surprising that they were the ones to have done so, since resource sharing and support for collection development were among RLG's highest priority goals. RLG's methods are embodied in its *Conspectus*,[2] which provides a structure for dividing collections by subject into 7,000 categories based on the Library of Congress classification schedules. To this is added a set of definitions for variations in collecting rates that go from buying virtually everything published in a subject area to buying solely the most general, landmark works or, if a subject is out of scope, buying nothing in that subject area at all. The *Conspectus* structure and definitions furnish an objective basis for comparing the existing collections of two or more libraries and finding them stronger or weaker depending on what the data reflect about current holdings as well as the projected future rate of collection in each subject area.

The *Conspectus*, because of its origins and intended use by RLG libraries, is necessarily geared toward large research collections. However, other library cooperatives made up of nonresearch libraries, realizing the value of objective collection data to support coordinated collection development, have adapted *Conspectus* methodology to their different needs and purposes. In 1986, the Library and Information Resources for the Northwest cooperative (LIRN) reported success in using an adaptation of the *Conspectus* that enables libraries to choose between two smaller sets of broader categories as well as the full 7,000 divisions.[3] Its experiences are being duplicated by other ventures among library cooperatives in the United States and abroad.[4]

Even without the *Conspectus* structure, however, libraries can agree to set goals of purchasing materials for joint use.

There are different ways to accomplish the goals. Subject areas can be divided and responsibilities assigned to individual members of the group, portions of individual members' budgets can be set aside for joint collecting by a body created for that purpose, or other strategies can be devised. No matter what joint goals and objectives are set and no matter what strategies are employed to meet them, those who make the decisions for the libraries involved and for the cooperative entity, if one is established, must be in agreement about the ultimate value of the joint project. If any decision maker believes his or her institution will be shortchanged in the venture, it probably will not succeed. And if any decision maker believes the results of the first few ventures into coordinated collection development have severely disadvantaged his or her library, it is unlikely that the library will continue to participate.

In the balance of this brief chapter, steps in the process of coordinating collection development are explored and discussed.

Which Libraries Might Benefit?

Libraries with mutual interests that are clear and specific are in a particularly good position to benefit from coordinated collection development, as are libraries that are units of one library system, libraries located within a small geographic area, and/or libraries with shared subject interest areas.

Library systems linked by a unifying administrative structure such as public libraries with a central unit and branches or academic libraries with departmental units, have much to gain from a coordinated collecting plan for some, if not many, of their materials. Managers at the top levels might be expected to be aware of overall patron needs and the relative strengths and weaknesses of collective holdings. The same unifying structure that provides system-wide administrative services might serve as a locus for coordinated collection development activity. Activities already in place might include such collection-related ones as coordinating orders, placing them jointly, receiving materials, cataloging them, and distributing them to the individual members.

Recent increases in interdisciplinary research in many subject areas may result in requests for the same titles by several departmental units in a college or university library system. These units could be duplicating titles that might be shared without hardship among several interested departments. In such an instance, the "system" can help to identify materials that qualify for such treatment and to determine which units are best suited to house them.

Libraries located within a small or well-defined geographic area may join together to share materials. If the libraries are near one another, patrons can use any of them with similar ease. If they are located at great distances from one another, transportation and communication strategies may be needed to speed delivery of materials from point to point, as, for example, the far-flung libraries of Alaska are doing with a statewide CD-ROM based catalog and airborne deliveries.

Although they may be helpful, administrative links are not a prerequisite for success. Coordinating collecting activities can benefit groups of libraries even if each one is completely independent administratively.

Groups of libraries with common areas of interest such as medicine, law, music, or art, frequently join forces to expedite interlibrary loans. If several medical libraries have different, well-defined specialties, each has something to gain by sharing materials in their areas of specialty with the others and receiving, in return, access to materials that may be requested occasionally, but are considered beyond the home library's collecting scope. The same may be true of other special libraries. However, merely because a group of libraries have common collecting interests or welcome interlibrary loans does not mean they will be able to coordinate their collection development activities. Attempts to combine the policies of profit-making firms with those of nonprofit institutions may not succeed. Barriers may arise from disparities in required budgeting and acquisition procedures or from other rules and regulations that conflict with commitments to the group effort such as a desire to keep activities confidential that could give away business secrets to competitors.

It is more difficult but not impossible for libraries with no administrative, subject, or geographic commonalities to succeed in coordinating their collection development programs. Impediments to success are the twin difficulties of formulating mutually agreeable goals and objectives, and communicating easily and rapidly both for decision making and for access to the shared materials.

What Decisions Must Be Made, and How?

The decision with the greatest impact on coordinated collection development is to engage in such a project at all, knowing that some measure of power and control over what may be purchased and how it will be acquired inevitably must be relinquished to the group. This may be the most difficult decision to be made by each of the participating libraries and to have approved by the library's governing body.

The second most important decision is how decisions relating to coordinated activities will be made. All decisions could be put to a vote of all participants, or delegated to some participants appointed to take responsibility for certain activities and charged with reporting to the group. Decisions might be made by a simple majority vote, or, if the participants so decide, by a specific proportion of votes, such as two-thirds or three-quarters of the members, or by consensus. What is most important is that the decision-making process is mutually agreeable and does not impede action. Requiring that all decisions be made unanimously might serve to prevent any action if it is difficult to arrange for votes or to obtain consent from some of the participants. On the other hand, leaving important decision making to one or two individuals might have results that the group as a whole would find objectionable, results that would be difficult to rescind after the fact, such as signing contracts or paying out funds.

Once the commitment to participate is made, approved, and a decision-making process accepted, the formulation of common goals and objectives will focus on the subject areas, languages, media, or other categories of materials that the coordinated effort will cover. Sometimes it is easier for libraries to identify the areas in which they do not wish to collaborate with others. Then the process of selecting areas for coordination consists of eliminating all of them and seeing what remains. However, a positive approach usually is preferable to a negative one.

Other decisions must be made on strategies for achieving the desired goals and objectives, including establishing a mutually agreeable, effective organizational structure. Rules must be adopted about its governance, funding, and staffing; devising methods of monitoring day-to-day activities; applying appropriate evaluative procedures; and methods of reporting progress regularly to the group. If a separate organization is created to carry out the joint program and a staff hired to operate it, decision making for day-to-day activities and non-policy issues might be delegated to a program manager who would be obliged to report to the group on a regular basis.

Decisions about a regular schedule of review and evaluation of activities, goals and objectives, policies, and operational procedures should be made at the outset, not instituted when or if a crisis is encountered. If both long- and short-range goals are set, they should be clearly distinguished and evaluated appropriately for their coverage and duration. Goals should be flexible enough to respond to important changes in the group or the environment. Unforeseen events and developments may require amendments to agreed-upon purposes, policies, or activities, and both the organizational structure and its decision processes should be capable of responding within reasonable periods of time.

Is a Formal Structure Necessary?

One method of ensuring that coordinated collecting activities do not suffer from lack of attention, funding, etc., is to establish a formal structure, a separate organization, charged with responsibility for the program. While it might be costly to do so, particularly at the beginning, creating a separate body and funding its staff and operations has several advantages:

1. Activities of the group effort can go forward without regard to demands on the time of the regular staff members in the individual libraries. If the group effort depends entirely on time contributed by staff members of the participating libraries, who are carrying group duties as an extra load in addition to their regular work, it may suffer whenever unforeseen exigencies take precedence. No matter how troubling, the time allotted to the group effort might have to be spent on local problems.
2. The coordinated collecting activity is bound to generate its own paperwork (the term "paperwork" does not refer only to paper-based records, but to records in any format), requiring its own space, equipment, etc.
3. If joint purchases of materials are to be made and/or housed for the group, establishing an entity to make the purchases and maintain the joint collection may be more efficient than parcelling out responsibilities among several participants, or expecting one library to shoulder the whole load.[5]
4. If the project involves purchase, maintenance, and/or administration of equipment and supplies such as computer hardware and software, etc., an organization to be responsible for these things is very important, if not absolutely necessary.
5. Establishing such an entity provides tangible evidence of commitment to the project on the part of the member libraries, which might prove helpful in seeking special funding.
6. Establishing a separate unit facilitates—indeed, requires—the appointment of personnel to support the project.

Despite the advantages of creating a separate unit to handle coordinated collecting activities, there is no requirement to do so. The primary disadvantage is the cost of establishing and maintaining the unit, which can be reason enough to prevent its creation.

When a separate unit is not established, group collecting activities may be based in one library or several, may be run by designated staff members in each of the individual libraries or by one or several of them, and decisions may be made at meetings where representatives of the participating libraries discuss issues and work out solutions. Even when a separate unit is created and an administrator selected to head it, representatives of each participating library probably would form an advisory or policy-making body to set or approve goals and objectives, monitor activities, and evaluate the unit's progress.

What Data Is Needed?

The data most needed to begin considering coordinated collection development goals and objectives are profiles of the libraries that wish to participate in the effort, i.e., comparative statistics about their users, funding, current holdings, usage of materials, and current collecting plans. Reliable reports of collection overlaps and duplicate holdings are important. Unique and common features of existing collecting policies and procedures, including the selection criteria being used by each library, need to be identified. Information about staffing and staff expertise also may be relevant, as may information about currently used vendors and the provisions of current contracts, including the distribution of discounts and surcharges. All of the data needs to be prepared for use in decision making, i.e., evaluated and organized in a useful manner.

Not only must it be possible to gather, evaluate, and organize relevant data effectively, the data must also be shared. One librarian may be surprised to find that another librarian considers certain types of data too sensitive to share, e.g., information about fund allocations or about staff expertise. It is not difficult to understand that data about collection, funding, or staffing weaknesses could be perceived as potentially embarrassing. But negotiation of subject areas or material types that would lend themselves to coordinated collecting depends on identification of such areas from the accumulated information. Decision-makers must be able to discern sufficient benefits for their institutions to repay them for relinquishing total control over future selection and acquisition in those areas, and it is hard data about money and materials that is most convincing.

Budget data, likely to be most sensitive of all, needs to be examined carefully and projected with caution, particularly when some of the funds are precommitted, or based on elements that can change rapidly, such as student registers or population. Funds that are not available for discretionary uses or that cannot be reallocated without approval by legislatures, courts, or other bodies need to be identified and, perhaps, omitted from consideration.

Steps in Implementation

1. The first step in implementing any collective plan must be to obtain commitments, preferably in writing, from the governing bodies of the participating libraries to work together on the coordinated collection development project. Documents framing the intent of the plan should be drawn up and signed, whether they take the form of legal contracts or statements of agreement on the overall undertaking. While the chief administrators of the participating libraries might be the persons authorized to sign the documents, it is the directors or trustees of the parent institutions, municipalities, agencies, or firms who, being ultimately responsible, should give their formal consent to the undertaking, right from the start.

2. Agreement on more specific long and short term goals and objectives is the next step, and should not be put off until organizational and administrative decisions are made. In fact, the types of organizational and administrative structures adopted should be geared to the kinds of goals chosen, particularly the long-term goals that the group decides it

wishes to accomplish. Ambitious goals may be ill-served by an invisible organization dependent on informal contributions of time and money. On the other hand, limited goals may not require investments in an elaborate formal structure requiring special staffing, housing, and equipment.

3. The next step is design of a suitable organizational structure and/or division of responsibilities among the participating libraries. Whether or not a special unit is created by the group, a legally binding contract should be drawn at this point, outlining specific contributions of money, staff, space, equipment, materials, etc. to be made by each member library. It should also set forth provisions concerning individual library operations that impact the collective effort. Materials and services to be furnished to each member library by the group also should be specified clearly. The authorities that govern each of the member libraries should be willing to sign the contract, binding themselves for the period of time covered by the contract to fulfill the obligations set by mutual agreement and to receive the benefits to which they are entitled.

4. Specific plans must now be made to carry out the goals and objectives to which the members have agreed. The agreed-upon structures for executing group activities must be put in place. If a special, separate unit is to be created and staffed, it must be done. If separate accounts for group funds are to be established, or contracts for equipment, supplies, and services negotiated, they must be executed. If an informal structure is to be the vehicle for the project, it must be initiated. A governing body of representatives from the member libraries should be formed. A project manager should be selected and charged with supervising or carrying on the day-to-day tasks of the project.

5. Specific, short-term objectives consistent with the overall goals of the group should be set and approved, assigned priorities, and strategies for meeting them devised for approval by the governing body. Specific objectives and strategies for their attainment may be developed by the governing body itself or by its designee, in all likelihood, the project manager. In the latter event, the governing body should have

the right to approve the objectives, their priorities, and the strategies to be implemented before work may begin. The specific objectives should be framed in measurable terms and carry a time limit, preferably no longer than a year, in contrast to the more general goals, which are likely to cover a much longer period of time. Alternative strategies to reach each objective should be developed along with the required inputs of money, staff, and time. Recommendations of the project manager should be considered carefully, but the final decisions should be the responsibility of the governing body.

6. Once objectives, priorities, and strategies are approved, the project manager should be allowed to take the reins and proceed with implementation of the plan. The project manager should have regular meetings with the governing body, presenting data that give a record of ongoing activities and operations, and taking the opportunity to ask questions, obtain approvals, or otherwise inform and communicate with the representatives of the group. If the project manager is chosen from among the staff members of the participating libraries, sufficient time should be scheduled for this person's coordinated collection development tasks, and responsibilities for tasks at his or her individual library assigned to others.

How Can Success Be Measured?

The best way to measure the success of the coordinated collection development venture is to evaluate it in the same manner as any individual library collection development cycle. Measurements of results of the coordinated activities must be matched against the desired objectives set at the start of the venture. If, for example, the objective was to establish a joint collection of 500 costly periodical titles, or to divide responsibility for collecting foreign language literatures, with each library taking over a particular language or country and purchasing all available literary materials for that language/country, it should be easy to determine whether the objective has been accomplished. In the first scenario, if the joint collection of periodicals contains only 350 periodicals, or, in the second scenario, if some of the libraries have not purchased available literary materials in their designated language or from the designated countries, then the acquisition of materials has not met the goals. Furthermore, if, as part of the agreement, criteria were set for the maximum length of time individual users might have to wait to obtain desired items and most of them have had to wait longer, one could conclude that service did not meet expectations, even if the materials were purchased.

If long-term goals were set that stretch over several years, reviews at the end of shorter periods, e.g., at the end of each quarter, semester, or year, usually are made. Performance is examined with an eye toward how closely progress at any particular point matches projections for that period, and whether it is sufficient to bring the project's ultimate goals within reach by the close of the entire period.

If progress has fallen short of expectations or exceeded them by large amounts, changes may be made to the plan to increase the likelihood of success or to raise the goals and objectives to match the greater potential being demonstrated. Such changes may take several forms, including altering inputs of money, staff, space, equipment, etc., or increasing or decreasing expected outcomes in terms of the amounts or kinds of materials acquired or the waiting time to obtain them from libraries other than the owning library, or both.

Conclusion

Coordinated collection development appears to be a valuable program through which libraries can deliver more materials to their users than their budgets would ordinarily allow, yet it should not be perceived as an all-good, all-powerful panacea to end all collecting problems. Several drawbacks should be clear from the foregoing discussion, including the need for individual libraries to give up control over some portions of their budgets and materials as well as their staff hours and, possibly, computing power, physical space, etc. The commitment to benefit the group may require changes in individual library collections and services that are seen as sacrifices on the part of librarians and members of the library's public. Decisions made by the group may not be interpreted universally as wise, advantageous, or feasible. Lack of adequate controls over implementation and day-to-day activities can result in failure to keep the project on course, and inability to reach the group's goals and objectives.

In addition to all of these caveats, there is the major issue of copyright law and the library's obligation to act lawfully with regard to the rights of the writers, artists, composers, publishers, etc. of the materials being purchased and used in a coordinated collection development program. It might be efficient to buy one copy of a title, digitize it, and deliver it to any requester, but this undoubtedly would be found to be illegal. The line between forms of sharing that are legal and forms that are not have yet to be defined for every form of resource sharing, but libraries have an obligation to refrain from those known to be illegal, or, for that matter, those known to be questionable.

In the long run, coordinated collecting will succeed where its goals and objectives are clear and precise and the librarians and other decision makers who control collecting decisions believe it can be made to work. Where intimate cooperation with outside institutions is viewed with suspicion or where librarians cannot articulate exactly what materials they wish to own and why, coordinated collection development is not likely to succeed—if it happens at all. Strategic planning for coordinated collection development requires commitment at top levels for its initiation and initial establishment, but it also requires commitment throughout the echelons of the participating libraries for its eventual implementation and accomplishment. That this can be done is clear from the experiences of the LIRN libraries, among others. Whether it can succeed in any particular group of libraries depends on the ability of the partners to do what must be done, as described above.

Suggestions for Additional Reading

Farrell, David. "The NCIP Option for Coordinated Collection Management," *Library Resources & Technical Services* 30 (Jan./Mar. 1986): 47–56.

Hewitt, Joe A. and John S. Shipman. "Cooperative Collection Development among Research Libraries in the Age of Networking." In *Advances in Library Automation and Networking* 1 (1987): 189–232.

Kruger, Karen. *Coordinated Cooperative Collection Development for Illinois Libraries*. 3 volumes. Springfield: Illinois State Library, 1982.

Mosher, Paul H. "Cooperative Collection Development Equals Collaborative Interdependence." In *Collection Management: Current Issues*. New York: Neal-Schuman Publishers, 1989.

Resource Sharing & Information Networks. Quarterly publication edited by Robert M. Holley; published by Haworth Press.

Standards for Cooperative Multitype Library Organizations. Prepared by the Association of Specialized and Cooperative Library Agencies. Chicago: American Library Association, 1990.

Beyond the Nineties: The Electronic Library and Technical Services

by Pamela Reekes McKirdy

The concept of the "electronic library" has been explored by many and has come to symbolize the view of the library of the future incorporating technological innovation, a broad interpretation of what constitutes information to be provided, and myriad electronic interconnections. Since the impact on technical services derives from the nature of end user services, the ways in which the library of the future will serve its users must be explored before the effect on technical services can be gauged. In so doing, an approximate time frame must be established for the inquiry. Close enough to be forecast with some confidence and sufficiently removed to be useful, the first decade of the new millennium is the chronological setting for this view of the future.

Details of a Future Scenario

The electronic library may be conceived as the set of sources and services used by an individual in acquiring information from anywhere via a personal electronic workstation or as a physical library whose services are supported by electronic devices. Although some may find the former to be an attractive scenario, the latter is in evidence already, closer to being a reality, and sufficiently challenging as a topic for examination. Therefore, a physical plant, a staff, a collection of resources, a set of services, operational functions, and a definable user base is assumed.

The library of one or two decades hence is likely to be very much like the library of today, though physical changes will have been made to improve the conditions for retention of paper materials and the equipment necessary to provide broader availability. The archival function will not be abandoned in the twenty-first century, and preventative and restorative preservation of materials will be accepted practice. The library building will house many types of materials, but shelves of books will continue to predominate; it is unlikely that a more efficient packaging (relatively cheap, portable, and requiring no equipment to use) will replace books during this period. Microform storage and equipment for use will be conveniently accessible since much of the preservation effort of the future, like that of today, will use this relatively inexpensive and reliable technology.

Equipment for use with nonbook materials will be evident, often in use, and kept in good repair. Video viewing stations will be popular with an ever more visually oriented audience. Archives of recreational and documentary films will be distributed via videodisks usable with both simple players and computers. As aural and visual materials are incorporated into more of the educational curriculum and are used as integral components of interactive computer-assisted instruction, people will expect to find information expressed in more ways than print. Collections of slides and pictures, available now only to those who own or house them, will be reproduced and indexed, and made widely available. To support access to a wide variety of information ranging from local networks and information files to international resources in print, picture, sound, and video, computer workstations will be numerous and scattered throughout the library. These workstations will provide the means for selecting, viewing, listening, and copying segments of the resources discovered to add to personal files for later review or incorporation into individual multimedia presentations. Study areas will be provided, but carrels will be wired for electricity and communications and some will include hardware as well. Document delivery will extend well beyond the library walls and will include provision of nonbook format materials. Small branch mini-libraries will be established wherever they might be needed, e.g., in or near classrooms, offices, dormitory rooms, and other residences, employing clusters of terminals so that computer-based information may be used.

Technological advances are progressing at a rate far more rapid than would have been expected ten or twenty years ago, and there is little doubt that most options librarians wish to pursue in the creation, dissemination, or use of information will be adequately supported technologically. Advances in software concepts have been as rapid as development of hardware to support them and it is impossible to forecast new concepts that may spring from the availability of newer, more powerful machines. It is difficult enough attempting to determine the extent to which currently available technology will be adopted in information-based activities.

Computer-based technical services modules supporting ac-quisitions, serials check-in, and binding control will lessen the tedium of repetitive tasks required in performing these functions, and provide better and more timely information to both staff and users. Use of bibliographic utilities such as OCLC, RLIN, Utlas, or WLN will expand through the devel-opment of products based on CD-ROM data storage. Use of reference databases in this format also is growing; online services will expand into full text for some sources and develop alternative user interfaces. Online catalogs housed on mainframe computers, minicomputers, or microcompu-ters (with and without CD-ROM) will be developed, allowing use from numerous points inside and outside the library. Computer manipulated indexes and processing will provide retrieval by keywords, allow the use of logical operators, and indicate location and circulation status for items in library collections. Circulation systems will mature and be inte-grated with other functional modules. Future library auto-mation will provide more efficient and refined systems to perform technical functions, but innovations will be most apparent in two major areas: information available to the user and the nature of the user interface.

As libraries convert paper records into computer-based records, they acquire more than the capability of providing an online catalog; they develop the means to share information about what they have with other libraries and agencies. Networks of libraries historically have grouped themselves to share resources and work cooperatively. Some libraries have clustered to build and share an online catalog cooperatively. Telecommunications networks and software products (e.g., IRVING, a networking software package) have been developed to allow users of one OPAC to search another directly with familiar commands and displays even if the software vendors supplying the OPACs differ. The Linked Systems Project of the Library of Congress (LSP) is working to facilitate the sharing of data and authority records between unlike computer systems. LSP uses the developing OSI standard. It is feasible to expect that future library users will be able to take advantage of these expanded search capabilities to see what is available in other libraries.

The role of the academic library versus that of the campus computer facility is being examined in many institutions and, in some places, they are being merged. The differences between their roles as providers of information have become difficult to identify and, as free text becomes more widely available, the distinction will blur still further. Libraries will acquire bibliographic, full text, and numerical data files from vendors who ordinarily supply services online so that local search and retrieval may be offered. The data may be in CD-ROM or the database may be mounted on local mainframe computers. Access today is primarily through a separate interface than that used for the catalog, but a decade or two hence, it may be as easy as choosing a menu option from an expanded version of the initial login screen.

Electronically updated materials and services (e.g., databases such as LEXIS and NEXIS) and electronically published "journals" form another core information service to be provided by the library. The provision of new information resources is being undertaken by some libraries and the availability of the new census data in computer-based form is challenging some libraries to deal with primarily numerical data. Since support for use of information often falls to the provider, libraries are likely to take on more end user training and assistance in both the selection and manipulation of information in many forms.

Once libraries have assumed responsibility for providing numerous varied information resources, they will be faced with the task of simplifying and integrating the ways in which representations of those resources may be retrieved and assessed, and the materials themselves examined. Libraries have already begun to integrate bibliographic citations from various sources with traditional catalog entries and include, as well, descriptions of articles, computer files, pictures, equipment, artifacts, and full text of some documents. With the MARC format for bibliographic data already applied to other kinds of data (e.g., authority data, classification entries) and expanded to encompass any kind of item description, one can imagine a virtual "universal information catalog," which, if not restricted by cost or size, could allow anyone to obtain any information resource. Acquisition could be immediate if online full text is supported or requested through other document delivery channels.

Current Trends Supporting the Future Scenario

The whole range of information resources described above actually is available now, but it cannot be obtained easily or economically. The end user can consult bibliographic sources in print, CD-ROM, online, or use an intermediary to do so. Full text may be available in computer-based form or in print, but the end user may have to wait for interlibrary loan procedures to deliver it in, most likely, printed or printout form. What is technically and economically achievable over the next several years are improvements in the process of obtaining information. These improvements will make it possible to obtain wanted information more rapidly, with less intellectual effort, and in the most effective physical forms.

Integrating the presentation of information in many formats and from a variety of sources in a uniform catalog interface for end users will come primarily from software developments. Merging data from different storage devices (e.g., CD-ROM, videodisk, remote mainframe files, local mini-computer disks), translation of protocols between systems, and mapping of data from one vendor's format to that of another will be achieved through programming. The linking of systems, however, yields only part of the improvement in end user support. To provide optimal service, the user interface itself must be improved. Graphical User Interfaces (GUIs) as implemented in the Apple Macintosh and DOS Windows environments offer an opportunity to move beyond the less friendly verbal Menu and Command modes. Some vendors already are exploring windowing options. Librarians are experimenting with the development of Macintosh-based interfaces using Apple's HyperCard product. As users become accustomed to these interfaces in their other computing, they will come to expect them in the library's computer systems. The very attractive features of multiple windows, choice of functions through graphics, ability to move through multiple levels of system hierarchy (called "hyperjumps"), and potential integration of remote information functions with local user processing, make this a likely development in future library systems.

Apple's HyperCard is already gaining acceptance in the library community, although other products offer similar features and prospects. Librarians are using this flexible program package to design and execute new strategies for conveying information about the library and its resources. Because HyperCard allows great flexibility in designing content links, provides easy import and export of data from a variety of devices (audio, video, CD-ROM, modems, etc.), allows development of a simple-to-use interface, and is a productive programming tool, its use is spreading rapidly. Helpful, too, is a marketing strategy that bundles HyperCard with the purchase of Macintosh hardware. Competitive products offer some alternative or additional features, but the concept of the application is the important point. Since HyperCard stacks (i.e., program modules) are easily modified, they are versatile interface design tools that could help bring about library-specific and user-tailored systems. Although there are difficulties inherent in a user-modifiable interface, the problems are not specific to the library setting and solutions may be expected to be devised.

If users are provided with a single familiar interface for personal files, library files, and other applications, they can move freely between internal and external files. Currently, end users carry away citations from CD-ROM databases on a disk to load into personal files on other computers. Products are available that allow downloading of bibliographic data from OCLC or RLIN into other citation formats (e.g., into the University of Chicago or Modern Language Association style), and personal bibliographic management software readily translates citations from one standardized format to another. The ability to download numerical data to spreadsheet templates and to download textual data to commercially marketed word processing packages or database managers will be made available to end users and can be expected to be supported by libraries in the not-too-distant future. (If libraries were to be the sole beneficiaries of these provisions, it is unlikely that they would be forthcoming soon. What gives credence to the prediction is that others are designing just such links for applications in education and business. Their efforts should provide good models for the development of better interface designs, data transfer routines, and tutorials and other help facilities.)

The combination of integrated availability of local and remote information files from a variety of sources coupled with an easy-to-use interface that supports graphics, sound, text, and downloading to personal files will be attractive to the library's end users and is technologically feasible. Although innovations may supersede the products and machines of today, the integration of sources and interface is a goal which is likely to be pursued by libraries until achieved.

The Potential of Artificial Intelligence

The effects of techniques of artificial intelligence and expert systems on the library systems of tomorrow are far from clear. In more advanced scenarios, computers would process natural language queries (even those posed vocally), determine likely information sources, gather data, analyze it, prepare it, and respond in natural language (again, perhaps by means of a spoken reply). The ability of computers to recognize varying voice input of more than a few dozen words or to process natural language unambiguously has yet to be achieved and, although computer-gathered data from varied databases using thesaurus terms may be possible, computer analysis still is quite limited. That is not to say that someday we may not have intelligent personal information systems, but the time is unlikely to be near.

There are, however, ways in which artificial intelligence may aid in the provision of library services. Research on natural language processing will allow library catalogs to be more powerful and sensitive in processing queries, although human judgment still will be required to assess the results. Programming that includes logical rules and fuzzy matching algorithms will also improve catalog performance and enhance the nature of responses to queries. Systems which do phonetic matching, thesaurus lookups, and weighting of input and response terms already have incorporated the beginnings of intelligence into library applications. The future user interface may include provision for user-specified incorporation of a range of features drawn from artificial intelligence developments and imposed from the personal point of view (e.g., using citation relevance feedback from the individual to build a personalized weighted term index filter). Robotics may be employed in physical activities such as material storage and retrieval. Image scanning and optical character recognition may be used more widely than today if it becomes less costly and more reliable.

Artificial intelligence features are not a panacea, but they may serve well as aids to human intellectual efforts.

Technical Services in the Future Scenario

With these images of library end user service in the future, various areas of technical services can be examined to see what problems, prospects, and issues are likely to emerge.

ACQUISITIONS AND COLLECTION MANAGEMENT

The acquisition system of the future will include features that are becoming available today, but they will be better integrated into the local system and they will exploit communications links with other systems and sources. Items to be acquired will be determined by the same means as they are now, since human review and judgment are necessary in making collection development decisions. Information to support the decision-making process may, however, be generated from use statistics (e.g., circulation, holds placed), lists of unsuccessful queries of the catalog, online requests placed by end users and staff, postings from publishers and jobbers that match specific subject and audience profiles, or electronic postings from fellow consortium members. It will be possible to build a file of searches using standard numbers which will result in automatic query of databases for reviews, publisher data, and the MARC record(s) for each item so that selection decisions may be effected more easily. The decision to acquire a title will be reflected immediately in the library's catalog, and status information will be posted as available. Orders for materials will be transferred via telecommunications to publisher, jobber, or other vendor.

Clearly, if this scenario is to emerge, work must proceed toward universal adoption of standard identifiers (e.g., ISBN, SAN), which may serve as retrieval elements for a variety of systems. Widespread adoption of such standards requires the cooperation of librarians, publishers and producers, bibliographic utilities, database vendors, government agencies, and others. Implementation for titles in all physical forms must be effected if standard numbers are to be relied on as unique identifiers for all acquired materials. Point of capture (the point at which a record is printed or downloaded), for MARC records may be moved to the acquisitions process, as many libraries already are doing; provision of information about on-order and in-process materials (even with unverified cataloging) will be much enhanced.

Selection of materials will become more difficult in the future whether or not sophisticated selection and acquisitions systems are available. The availability of multiple formats for many titles and the ephemeral nature of some data and reports may require innovative strategies for local retrieval, display, storage, and distribution. As the cost of acquiring, preserving, and storing print materials continues to rise and nonprint materials (e.g., CD-ROMs and videodisks) become more readily acceptable, decisions about what should be acquired may necessitate coordination with other internal and external agencies. Shared collection development will be more widespread and institutions will consider carefully what should be housed at the library for immediate use.

Selection will include decisions about materials to be made available via online and local systems. There are costs associated with the searching, viewing, and downloading of information (citations and data). Budget allocations will become very complex and will require balancing the amounts expended for online viewing, borrowing, and acquisition. Libraries already have had to grapple with how to pay for online searches, CD-ROM products, and local databases; in the future, the problem will be more extensive and complicated. Librarians must work with vendors to develop pricing structures that are fair to end users as well as to the vendors, and which protect intellectual property rights.

With such complex decisions to be made, evaluation must be ongoing. Computer systems can generate statistics on various activities, files, indexes, and users, but librarians will have to develop strategies for monitoring statistics that are meaningful to the local context. Services must be designed for the user clientele and decisions about acquisition, borrowing, and online viewing must be evaluated to optimize overall expenditures. Studies using sampling techniques, statistical analyses, and other research methods will be required to determine the appropriateness of alternate efforts. Automated systems can support such studies through programs that allow specification of data collection from the system and which will provide for data transfer directly into spreadsheets and statistical analysis packages. The library's usual services will have to be expanded even as ever-present budget limitations must be met. Therefore, studies of end user populations will be essential and ongoing in the attempt to provide more rapid availability of relevant materials at acceptable costs.

PRESERVATION MANAGEMENT

Preservation of paper material will continue and use of acid paper will decline. Microfilm will continue to serve as an archival medium since even ten or twenty years hence no one will be certain that other media are as reliable. Microform sets will be marketed with the associated access data (computer-based cataloging, indexing, authority records) included. Popular items may be reproduced from microforms onto machine-searchable videodisk "libraries" for easier use. Imaging and audio technologies will be used to reproduce, provide indexing for, and disseminate local collections of slides, recordings, and videorecordings as institutions incorporate these resources and attempt to preserve the original materials.

Preservation of materials will take on a new meaning as technological changes render today's machinery obsolete. Backward compatibility cannot be maintained indefinitely and files created today will require translation to new formats (both in terms of data structures and physical media) if they are to continue to be usable. Already, some libraries have computer files and applications which require machines that are no longer sold or supported by vendors; many librarians are concerned that today's machines will soon be outmoded. Decisions will have to be made as to what will be preserved (both machinery and computer-based data), what will migrate to new technology, and what will be discarded. Records management techniques will aid in determining retention of computer-based ephemera such as locally prepared databases, compilations, spreadsheets, numerical files, and other resources as well as more formally published files.

CATALOGING, CLASSIFICATION, AND INDEXING

Cataloging and indexing data will be readily available for most materials. Responsiblity for creating cataloging and indexing could shift to the publisher or producer, who would provide or contract for cataloging to be available in the publishing house's own database or in the bibliographic utilities. Cataloging and indexing will include more information than currently is provided, as descriptors, abstracts, tables of contents, and other strategies are employed to enhance retrieval. Some materials will be available in computer-based full text appended to the cataloging record itself. Cataloging records will be accompanied by the appropriate authority records to facilitate cross referencing, and some cataloging for items will consist of families of records to provide access to included works, articles, etc. The MARC record structure will be expanded to allow mapping of data elements for describing and indexing any kind of item; systems will support import and export of the evolved MARC communications format.

Some local materials and many items acquired from other countries will require local cataloging and indexing, but expert systems for automatic cataloging will aid in the process through use of optical character recognition and sophisticated data analysis. Expert catalogers will review, verify, and correct the records. Cataloging tools will be available in computerized form as online files or in CD-ROM libraries with user-adaptable interfaces that allow consultation via multiple windows of the prevailing rules for description, subject vocabularies, and classification schedules at the same time one is viewing bibliographic and authority data.

The catalog interface will include one level at which the end user is guided through the classification and subject term indexes. The bases for this and other, more advanced interface levels, are the computer-based versions of the schedule or list and the interface software, which will be available in a locally modifiable form so that staff may add explanations, references, help modules, and tutorials.

Catalogers will apply their knowledge and organizational skills by serving as database consultants, designing and creating databases for others, and training people in the development and use of data files. End users will look for support in downloading citations, text, and data into standard applications such as databases and spreadsheets, or bibliographic, numeric, and graphics files, and moving data between software packages. Data transfer utilities will be more widely available in response to demands from the business sector, but some support also will be required for local library users. Some locally created files will be treated as part of the library's collection and citations for them (or the full data files) will be incorporated into the catalog. Authority work and indexing will be required for these materials, too.

Products culled from subsets of the available information and local resource files will be designed by library staff, who will need to be familiar with indexing terminology, record structures, screen and report format design, and the needs of end user populations. Subject specialists/bibliographers will team up with organization specialists to develop these, or libraries may reorganize along the lines of the Gorman model of subject specialist with both kinds of skills, unfettered by departmental distinctions in order to support such efforts.

DOCUMENT DELIVERY; CIRCULATION AND INTERLIBRARY LOANS

Document delivery will take many forms, most of which are already available. Print materials will continue to be common, but microforms will be used to provide access to much of the printed material published in the twentieth century. Many more sources will be provided directly in computer-based form, either as an option or as the sole format. Aural and visual information will be included, so workstations and other input-output devices must support user viewing, listening, and downloading of the various formats. Some users may need to convert printed text into digitized text or it may be necessary to do so for resource sharing, so scanning and optical character recognition services will be found within some libraries.

The catalog will provide the means for finding available information resources in a tiered fashion. Within a first tier cluster, response will have to be most immediate; remote sources for computerized forms also will be expected to be obtainable rapidly. Other physical delivery paths most likely will remain as they are today, e.g., facsimile transmission and postal services.

"Document" delivery will not consist solely of print analogs, but will include downloadable textual, numerical, and graphic information, and other resources. End users will expect transportability into a variety of computer applications and software formats for immediate use and integration with other data. Libraries will provide consultation and training in use of telecommunications and file transfers, as well as other technical topics.

Circulation systems today are well automated, but future systems will include enhancements permitting automatic generation of electronic mail (email) notices to clients with overdue materials or to clients for whom materials have been received. Catalog queries may evolve from simple searches with the ability of placing holds on local materials to placing interlibrary loan requests directly and incorporating downloaded search results directly in online reference consultations. Statistics on catalog-provided use of citations and full text will be merged with more traditional counts to aid in the analysis of collection use as librarians try to optimize services.

RESOURCE SHARING AND COORDINATED COLLECTION DEVELOPMENT

Resource sharing will be achieved more easily and quickly. Facsimile transmission with optical character recognition software will be readily available for shorter textual documents so they may be transmitted and/or converted into digitized text. Full text available online may be downloaded within the restrictions developed to accommodate intellectual property regulations and cost constraints. Other materials may be physically transferred through means similar to today's arrangements.

Library networks will reflect tiered arrangements already becoming established (e.g., local, within-state region, state, regional resource libraries, national, and international) and will support extensive resource-sharing efforts. Special interest networks (e.g., subject-oriented, language-oriented, kind of industry) also will serve to cluster libraries for resource and information sharing. Requests for materials will follow preestablished network pathways designed to make resource transfer efficient and to balance allocations. Compensation will be provided to remunerate the net lenders, but access to materials generally will not be denied on the basis of inability to pay.

Shared collection development will be implemented within the smaller clusters being established today. Small collections will be banded together, basic core collections will be maintained at appropriate locations, and specialized resources will be distributed within the organizational cluster. In educational institutions, some courses will be clustered at individual schools, so collection support will mirror the allocation of faculty (this is a strategy to avoid stresses associated with the decline in available faculty predicted to occur around the mid-nineties). Since the materials will not be solely printed book materials, coordination will require greater technical skill and support. Shared acquisitions and catalogs must be accompanied by closer institutional ties, effective staff cooperation, and responsive communications systems. Statistical data will be generated and analyzed to gauge the efficacy of resource allocations and the sharing of information and materials. Aggregate data will be useful in determining query pathways and in calculating appropriate remuneration for the holders of intellectual propery rights and institutional net lenders.

At higher level tiers, resources also will be shared and collection development responsibilities allocated on the model of the Research Libraries Group. Internationally, bibliographic agencies will take responsibility for primary collection of materials by and about political, language, and cultural groups. Overlaps still will exist, however, since many materials apply in a variety of contexts and redundancy is necessary to ensure ready availability and the survival of materials. International technological and bibliographic standards become essential elements in such a scenario and must be developed. Obviously, this effort will be of longer duration than one or two decades.

Conclusion

Is the scenario above likely to be in place by the turn of the century? Probably not, since the process of change in libraries (as in society) is slow—evolutionary, not revolutionary. Systems will continue to improve as technological innovations are diffused into the library sector, but people must adapt and several problems require resolution before implementation of universal access and resource sharing can occur.

Technical difficulty in linking systems physically and through software must be overcome. As efforts are undertaken to connect existing networks, products are being developed to bridge the gap between extant protocols, e.g., between TCP/IP and OSI/X.25, and among various online catalog products.

The current solutions are likely to be satisfactory for the short term only, since translations and crossovers add to processing time and contribute to delays in response time. Work to develop common standards, however, is not easy and involves significant negotiation; and when completed, more time is required for implementation. The impact of hardware incompatibility seems, as one reads the journals, to lessen as time goes on, but it is a very real problem to the librarian who seeks to share an IBM-DOS file with a Macintosh user. With money and expertise the problem is trivial, but is there enough of either in libraries today to make one optimistic about the near term?

The advanced systems available now provide services which may approach those described here, but can most libraries afford today's technology? Will librarians be able and willing to pay for the technology of the twenty-first century? It will be possible to finance the libraries of the future only if strategies are developed today which target these goals for tomorrow. Whatever services seem most appropriate for the coming decades must be identified *now* if they are to be ready when they are wanted. Resource sharing may decrease costs to individual institutions so that a wider variety of information sources may be made available to the combined population, but it requires alterations to organizational structures, shifts in responsibility, reallocation of resources, and other adjustments which may alter individual library staffs and collections radically. Such change is not effected quickly or easily.

The debate over fees for service has yet to be resolved. As service options become more varied and complex and information is distributed more easily to the end user, better methods are needed to identify costs. If access to more information and expanded services is to be provided, some current resources will have to be sacrificed. Automation has never obviated staff; it will not do so in the future either. More sophisticated systems will require more assistance to end users, not less. If staff costs do not decline, what will? Sharing acquisition of materials may help in freeing money for searching broader information sources, but convenience in consulting those materials will vary, and, additionally, institutional autonomy will decline with cooperative efforts. It will be necessary to determine if these "costs" are acceptable and find ways to minimize them. Control of the charges for retrieval and use of information may be extremely difficult as end users communicate beyond their home library systems.

Today's pricing mechanisms are unlikely to serve well for future systems since they are primarily based on units used and reflect royalties developed in a print-oriented information economy. Payment schedules will have to be developed that allow libraries to plan budget allocations, but also adequately compensate database vendors, publishers, authors, and other information purveyors. Public libraries (and the library world in general) traditionally have attempted to avoid denying access to information because of inability to pay. As the applications of technology seem to further disadvange the "have-nots," the goal of freedom of access may become more of a responsibility for public institutions such as libraries. Ways will have to be found to subsidize services for those who cannot pay, and other users will have to recognize their responsibility to fund library activities through taxes, tuition, or direct fees.

Intellectual property laws require re-examination in light of new technologies. A major revision of the copyright law was passed in 1976, and revisions have been made to solve some of the problems resulting from new technology, but the law still reflects its origins in a non-electronic, print-oriented environment. It is unlikely that property rights will be protected adequately or users of the information well served by attempts to apply royalty provisions from book and journal agreements to online titles. With books and journals, one can view the text yet not be able to reproduce it easily; in the computer environment, downloading a file that is being sent to a computer for viewing is undetectable as well as uncontrollable. Technical protections seem only to invite ways to negate them (e.g., microcomputer copying programs and video signal unscramblers). New ways of compensating information creators and distributors are needed that are fair, but predictable, like the established prices for books and subscriptions for journals. The development of new pricing structures will necessitate much information gathering on retrieval and use, and will require a great deal of cooperation among concerned parties. This issue is unlikely to be resolved in the foreseeable future.

Changes in library services may be more gradual than indicated here, but immediate preparation is necessary if librarians are to exert any measure of control over the evolution rather than be driven by it. Even today, staff need ongoing education and training to administer current systems and support the information needs of contemporary end users. In anticipating the demands of the future, librarians must educate themselves and their staffs to be knowledgeable about technology and its impact on the library. Librarians must be ready to train and support end users in their information seeking and management activities and able to design and adapt systems responsive to their needs. Education and training are essential as old skills require translation into new skills.

In the early years of the twenty-first century, the library activities of acquiring, organizing, and delivering information resources to end users may not be so very different in concept from those of today, but perhaps librarians can derive greater satisfaction from being more effective in their efforts to bring information to people.

Appendix

The Survey: List of Participating Institutions and Survey Instrument

The libraries listed below responded to the survey on which this book is based, and permitted themselves to be identified. Thirteen more academic and fourteen more public libraries responded, too, but asked that their identities not be revealed. The balance of the responding libraries did not identify themselves, nor could they be identified as public or academic. (An asterisk denotes members of a selected control group of libraries.)

ACADEMIC LIBRARIES

Lurleen B. Wallace Library, Troy State University, Troy, Alabama
*Scripps Institution of Oceanography Library, University of California, La Jolla, California
University Library, University of California, San Francisco, San Francisco, California
University Library, University of Colorado at Colorado Springs, Colorado Springs, Colorado
S. H. Coleman Library, Florida A&M University, Tallahassee, Florida
Paul V. Galvin Library, Illinois Institute of Technology, Chicago, Illinois
*Brookens Library, Sangamon State University, Springfield, Illinois
The Library, Wentworth Institute of Technology, Boston, Massachusetts
George C. Gordon Library, Worcester Polytechnic Institute, Worcester, Massachusetts

Oakland University Libraries, Oakland University, Rochester, Michigan

U. S. Conn Library, Wayne State College, Wayne, Nebraska

Lamson Library, Plymouth State College, Plymouth, New Hampshire

General Library, University of New Mexico, Albuquerque, New Mexico

Louis L. Manderino Library, California University of Pennsylvania, California, Pennsylvania

H. M. Briggs Library, South Dakota State University, Brookings, South Dakota

PUBLIC LIBRARIES

City of Cerritos Public Library, Cerritos, California
*Riverside City and County Public Library, Riverside, California
Charlotte-Glades Library System, Port Charlotte, Florida
Waterloo Public Library, Waterloo, Iowa
Campbell County Public Library, Cold Spring, Kentucky
*Ventress Memorial Library, Marshfield, Massachusetts
*Hennepin County Library, Minnetonka, Minnesota
Washington County Library System, Greenville, Mississippi
Manchester City Library, Manchester, New Hampshire
*The Free Library of Philadelphia, Philadelphia, Pennsylvania
Orangeburg County Library, Orangeburg, South Carolina
Rockingham Public Library, Harrisonburg, Virginia
*Tacoma Public Library, Tacoma, Washington

Glossary of Acronyms
and Selected Terms

This glossary is a compilation of acronyms used in the book with their spelled out equivalents as well as a selection of less familiar terms with definitions. Although most of the entries in the glossary are spelled out or defined when they are mentioned in the text for the first time, they are used subsequently without further explanation. Thus, for the reader who prefers to skip around the text, or who may have forgotten where a desired definition is located, this glossary will be helpful. In addition, a few terms from the general library literature on the topic of technical services are included even though they are not used in this book.

AACR *Anglo-American Cataloguing Rules*.

AACR1 *Anglo-American Cataloging Rules*, 1st edition, published in two versions, the North American text and the British text, both in 1967.

AACR2 *Anglo-American Cataloguing Rules*, 2nd edition, published in 1978.

AACR2R *Anglo-American Cataloguing Rules*, 2nd edition, 1988 revision.

ALA   American Library Association.

ALCTS   Association for Library Collections and Technical Services, a division of **ALA**. *See also* **RTSD**.

ALISE   Association for Library and Information Science Education.

APPLE II   A line of computer models produced by the Apple Corporation.

ARL   Association of Research Libraries.

AUTHORITY CONTROL   The process of ensuring that headings in the library catalog conform to authorized forms, usually involving maintaining records documenting the authorized forms and identifying unauthorized forms for which cross references will be created.

AUTHORITY FILE   A list of authorized headings, documentation, and cross references.

BARCODE   A computer-readable label in which alternating black and white bars represent numbers or other characters used to identify the items on which they are used. Also called ZEBRA LABELS.

BBOARD   Electronic bulletin board.

BIBLIOGRAPHIC DATABASE   A computerized compilation of bibliographic information, such as a library catalog or union list.

BIBLIOGRAPHIC CONTROL   The process of managing library materials by recording identifying data for each item and organizing it for retrieval in a desired manner. In U.S. libraries, bibliographic control is exercised through catalogs and bibliographies that identify materials and group them by authors, titles, and/or subjects.

BIBLIOGRAPHIC NETWORK   A group of libraries, linked by a computer network, that share bibliographic data.

BIBLIOGRAPHIC UTILITY   A large computerized network that appears to generate bibliographic records in much the same way electric utilities generate electricity. The growth of bibliographic records in the database usually is the result of contributions of original cataloging by the network's constituents.

BISAC   Book Industry Systems Advisory Committee.

BRS   Bibliographic Retrieval Service, an information system that furnishes access to a variety of databases for a fee.

CAN   *Conservation Administration News.*

CCS   Cataloging and Classification Section.

CD-ROM   Compact Disk-Read Only Memory.

CEO   Chief executive officer.

CHARGING   Checking out a library item, such as a book. *See also* DISCHARGING.

CLSI   A vendor of computer systems for libraries. The acronym has had different meanings over the years.

COMMAND MODE   In computing, an environment that requires users to enter commands in order to operate programs or manipulate data.

CONVERSION   *See* RETROSPECTIVE CONVERSION.

COPY CATALOGING   Cataloging by copying entirely or editing an existing record from a bibliographic database, and incorporating it into one's own catalog.

CPU   Central Processing Unit, the "core" work unit of a computer.

DDC   Dewey Decimal Classification.

DDC 20   Dewey Decimal Classification, 20th edition.

DIALOG   The commercial firm that functions as an information broker, providing access to hundreds of bibliographic and/or full text databases for a fee. Also, the database system of the firm. Originally part of the Lockheed Corporation, DIALOG is now a separate corporation.

DISCHARGING Checking in a returned library item, such as a book. *See also* CHARGING.

DOS Disk Operating System. The operating system common to IBM and IBM-compatible microcomputers.

DOS WINDOWS A software package that enables the user to view different parts of the programming in small sectors called "windows."

EDUCOM A nonprofit, educational networking organization that promotes sharing of computer resources.

EMAIL Electronic mail. A system of computer software and hardware through which users can send and receive electronic messages.

ENCAPSULATION Complete enclosure of a document in protective plastic covers designed to prevent further deterioration.

END USER The person for whom information is intended, in contrast with the person assisting her or him in obtaining the information.

FAX Facsimile, a form of electronic communication of information.

FUNCTION KEY A special key on a computer keyboard that is programmed to execute a series of commands when it is pressed.

GATEWAY Part of one computer system that connects it to other computer systems or to a telecommunications network through which other computers may be accessed.

GUI Graphical User Interface. A computer-user interface that employs visual icons in place of textual commands or menus.

HARDWARE Computer equipment.

HVAC The systems that control heating, ventilation, and air conditioning in a library.

HYPERMEDIA Interactive items based on large amounts of prerecorded information in audio, visual, and/or textual form, often in video and/or optical disk formats, with computer software that permits a user to make requests and receive responses. *See also* MULTIMEDIA.

IBM-PC International Business Machines-Personal Computer. A line of personal computers produced by the International Business Machines Corporation.

IFLA International Federation of Library Associations and Institutions.

ILL Interlibrary loan.

INFORMATION BROKER A person or group whose function is to purvey access to online bibliographic databases and/or the full text of informational materials and/or other services involving information, generally for a fee.

INPUT/OUTPUT DEVICE A piece of equipment whose function is to allow the entry of information into a computer and/or to allow the production of information from a computer, e.g., keyboards, touch sensitive screens, printers.

INTEGRATED SYSTEM A computer system that performs more than one function (usually, of technical services, such as cataloging and acquisition, or cataloging and circulation).

INTERFACE The point of interaction between person and computer or between two computers, and the method by which interaction is effected. Also called USER INTERFACE.

I/O Input/Output.

ISBD International Standard Bibliographic Description.

ISBN International Standard Book Number.

ISO/OSI *See* OSI.

ISSN International Standard Serial Number.

JSC *See* JSCAACR.

JSCAACR Joint Steering Committee for Revision of AACR.

KEYBOARDER Data entry staff.

KEYBOARDING The act of entering data into a computer through a keyboard.

LAN Local Area Network.

LC Library of Congress.

LCC Library of Congress Classification.

LCSH *Library of Congress Subject Headings*.

LIBRARY SYSTEM A group of libraries that are linked administratively. A library system may consist of a central library and branches or a number of co-equal agencies.

LIBS 100 The name of the computer system marketed by CLSI.

LINKING AUTHORITY CONTROL RECORDS The process of joining files containing authorized headings and bibliographic records. If authority and bibliographic records are linked in a computer system, the computer can verify that only valid headings are used. Without computers and linked records, all verification and validation must be done by hand.

LIRN Library and Information Resources for the Northwest.

LOCAL AREA NETWORK A network of computers, usually within a limited geographic location.

LOCAL NETWORK A small number of libraries, usually within a limited geographic area, sharing one computer system or having several computers linked with a local area network.

LOCAL SYSTEM A computer system designed to perform functions such as acquisitions, serials control, cataloging, catalog display, etc., wholly under the control of one library

or a small group of libraries, in contrast to larger BIBLIO-
GRAPHIC NETWORKS or BIBLIOGRAPHIC UTILITIES.

LSP   Linked Systems Project. A project of the Library of
Congress and bibliographic networks to link their diverse
computer systems.

MACINTOSH   A line of computer models produced by the
Apple Corporation.

MANUAL SYSTEM   An umbrella term for systems that are
not based on computers.

MARC   MAchine Readable Cataloging.

MARC FORMAT   A set of protocols for identifying bibliographic information for computer communication, devised
by the Library of Congress.

MENU MODE   In computing, an environment in which
users operate programs and manipulate data by selecting
options from a menu.

MODULE   In a computer system, the set of programs and/or
equipment that enables a function to be performed.

MULTIMEDIA   Items consisting of more than one part
where the parts are not in the same physical format, especially combinations of video and/or optical disks and computer software, as well as the equipment needed to use
them.

NAF   Name Authority File, a list of authoritative headings
for persons and corporate bodies produced by the Library
of Congress.

NCIP   North American Collections Inventory Project.

NEDCC   Originally New England Documents Conservation
Center, now called the Northeast Documents Conservation
Center.

NET LENDER   A library that lends more documents to
other libraries than it borrows from them through interlibrary loan.

NISO National Information Standards Organization.

NUC *National Union Catalog.*

OCLC Originally Ohio College Library Center, the acronym now stands for Online Computer Library Center.

OCR Optical Character Recognition.

OFFLINE Work performed or stored apart from the main computer or the main memory of the computer; also, not computerized.

OLUC Online Union Catalog, OCLC's database of bibliographic records.

ONLINE DATABASE A compilation of data in computerized form.

ONLINE SERVICE A compilation of data, often a large number of separate databases, in computerized form located at a central computer or network headquarters, from which subscribers or members may access the data, usually for a fee.

OPAC Online Public Access Catalog. *See also* PAC.

ORBIT A commercially marketed system of online bibliographic databases, some of which include full text of the documents, marketed by the Systems Development Corporation.

OSI Open Systems Interconnection Reference Model, a standard of the International Standards Organization defining communication protocols for the interconnection of two differing computer networks.

OSI/X.25 *See* OSI.

PAC Public Access Catalog. *See also* OPAC.

PDP-11 A series of minicomputers built by the Digital Electronics Corporation.

PHASE BOX A protective enclosure for damaged library materials.

PRESERVATION MICROFILMING The process of putting the contents of deteriorating materials on microfilm to preserve them.

PROPRIETARY Wholly owned and controlled by the vendor or "proprietor."

RECON *See* RETROSPECTIVE CONVERSION.

REPROGRAPHICS The unit charged with responsibility for microforms.

RESERVE DESK [ROOM] In academic libraries, the place where reserve collections are charged out [housed].

RESERVES In academic libraries, a collection of specially designated materials allowed to be borrowed solely for brief periods, usually measured in hours; in public libraries, requests made by patrons for materials not available at the moment, also known as "holds."

RETROCON *See* RETROSPECTIVE CONVERSION.

RETROSPECTIVE CONVERSION The process of converting bibliographic information from card or book records to computerized records for materials already held in collections before computer cataloging began. Also called CONVERSION.

RH Relative humidity.

RLG Research Libraries Group.

RLIN Research Libraries Information Network.

RTSD Resources and Technical Services Division, a division of ALA which changed its name in 1990 to Association for Library Collections and Technical Services.

SAN Standard address number.

SC350 A microcomputer-based software package for OCLC libraries that executes functions of serials control.

SISAC Serials Industry Systems Advisory Committee.

SOFTWARE Programs that enable computers to perform processing operations.

SOFTWARE PACKAGES *See* SOFTWARE.

TCP/IP An electronic communications protocol used in computer networking.

TERMINAL A visual display of computerized material, data, etc.

T-SLIP Transaction slip, a slip on which the data for borrowing a library item by a patron is recorded.

TURNKEY SYSTEM A library computer system in which the vendor of the system provides everything needed for implementation, including hardware, software, basic installation, training, and maintenance. The only components not usually provided by the vendor are a site for the equipment and the database of bibliographic information for the library's holdings.

UBC Universal Bibliographic Control, a program of IFLA.

UDC Universal Decimal Classification.

USBE United States Book Exchange. (Now defunct)

USER-FRIENDLY [UNFRIENDLY, HOSTILE] Slang term for easy to use [difficult to use, terribly difficult to use].

USER INTERFACE *See* INTERFACE.

UTLAS Now no longer an acronym, but the company known as Utlas International, the acronym once stood for University of Toronto Libraries Automated System.

VIDEO DISPLAY TERMINAL *See* TERMINAL.

WLN Originally Washington Library Network, now stands for Western Library Network.

WORKSTATION A powerful microcomputer enhanced with additional equipment such as facsimile machines, video or CD-ROM equipment, etc.

ZEBRA LABEL *See* BARCODE.

Notes

INTRODUCTION

1. Maurice F. Tauber and associates, *Technical Services in Libraries: Acquisitions, Cataloging, Classification, Binding, Photographic Reproduction, and Circulation Operations* (New York: Columbia University Press, 1954), [3].
2. Irene P. Godden, ed., *Library Technical Services: Operations and Management* (Orlando, FL: Academic Press, 1984), xi.
3. Michael Gorman and associates, *Technical Services Today and Tomorrow* (Englewood, CO: Libraries Unlimited, 1990), 2–3.
4. Tauber, *Technical Services in Libraries*, 4.
5. When he was in charge of general service activities at the University of Illinois at Urbana-Champaign, Michael Gorman coined the phrase "compleat librarian" to describe librarians on his staff who performed tasks in both public and technical service areas. At the Simmons College Symposium, James Neal, then assistant dean in charge of reference and instructional services at Penn State University, described how dual-role librarians had solved the library's cataloger problem, stating: "The consolidation of the databases with which both [public and technical] service areas must work, and the automation of many public and technical services activities has enabled the distribution of the professional aspects of technical operations, and the recruitment of individuals to cataloging within the collection and service environment." James G. Neal, "The Evolving Public/Technical Services Relationship: New Opportunities for Staffing the Cataloging Function," in *Recruiting, Educating, and Training Cataloging Librarians: Solving the Problems*, eds.

Sheila S. Intner and Janet Swan Hill (Westport, CT: Greenwood Press, 1989), 112.

6. Tauber, *Technical Services in Libraries*, xi.

7. Gorman, *Technical Services Today and Tomorrow*, xv.

8. The report of the Task Force asserted that employers were generally disappointed with the size and quality of applicant pools for job vacancies, many of which had to be re-advertised. It also said that library school catalogs from ALA-accredited schools seemed to offer a limited number of cataloging courses. Regarding library school cataloging curricula, Sellberg supported the view expressed by the Task Force, demonstrating that cataloging curriculum has been shrinking over time; but Miksa challenged these conclusions in a carefully-documented examination of offerings whose scope included cataloging despite the fact that the word "cataloging" did not appear in their titles. Miksa found that if one also counted such courses, the proportion of curriculum devoted to cataloging actually had increased. See the following:

"CCS Task Force on Education and Recruitment for Cataloging Report, June, 1986," *RTSD Newsletter* 11, no. 7 (1986): 71–78.

Roxanne Sellberg, "The Teaching of Cataloging in U.S. Library Schools," *Library Resources & Technical Services* 32, no. 1 (Jan. 1980): 30–42.

Francis Miksa, "Cataloging Education in the Library and Information Science Curriculum," in *Recruiting, Educating, and Training Cataloging Librarians*, 273–97.

9. The discussions and new material from the symposium's oral presentations can be found in *Cataloging: The Professional Development Cycle*, eds. Sheila S. Intner and Janet Swan Hill (Westport, CT: Greenwood Press, 1991).

10. *American Library Directory*, 40th ed., 2 vols., ed. Jaques Cattell Press (New York: Bowker, 1986).

11. For a discussion of deeper meanings in these appellations, see Sheila S. Intner, "Interfaces: The Technical Services Mystique," *Technicalities* 7, no. 1 (Jan. 1987): 8–11.

CHAPTER 1: THE SETTING

1. The general descriptions of the survey population that follow include all 120 of the institutions selected to receive the survey questionnaire, i.e., both institutions whose librarians answered the questionnaire (some of whom elected to be identified and some of whom chose to remain anonymous) and those whose librarians failed to reply. Similarly, the profile of respondents includes all of those contacted, some of whom replied and some of whom did not.

2. The four-year baccalaureate had to be among the institution's offerings, but it did not have to be the only one. Some of the academic institutions surveyed also offered two-year programs leading to associate degrees or certificates and/or postbaccalaureate programs leading to master's and doctoral degrees.

CHAPTER 2: COMPUTING IN TECHNICAL SERVICES

1. Tauber, *Technical Services in Libraries*, [388]-89.
2. Richard W. Boss and Judith McQueen, "Automated Circulation Control Systems," *Library Technology Reports* 18 (Mar.–Apr. 1982): 125–26.
3. The idea behind a turnkey system was that the library could purchase the system and, when it was delivered, turn the key that unlocked the central processing unit and begin operating it immediately. This simplistic vision of computing skipped over a number of prerequisites to implementation that negated the reality of such happenings—principally providing the data necessary for processing to begin, installing the system, and training the staff. In addition, the computers themselves were not completely reliable, and librarians learned the hard way the meaning of terms common to computer jargon such as "downtime" and "backup."
4. Quasi-turnkey vendors is a term meaning companies whose product offerings might include several options from a minimum of just a software package, designed to run on standard computers that could be purchased from any hardware retailer, but with the requisite training to implement the software and its maintenance and ongoing development, to the traditional complete turnkey system, combining such standard hardware with the rest of the components.
5. These annual surveys appeared at different times in many publications, e.g., in *Library Systems Newsletter*, by editors Richard W. Boss and Judy McQueen, in *Library Technology Reports*, by different authors depending on the kind of computing being described, and in *Library Journal*, written by Joseph R. Matthews and other authors, to mention just a few.
6. The acronym CD-ROM stands for Compact Disk-Read Only Memory. CD-ROM disks are a method of storing digitized information on a rigid disk that a computer reads with a special scanning device. CD-ROM disks can hold more than 1,000 times as much data on a single disk as the typical microcomputer floppy disk of the same size, enabling medium-sized libraries to store their entire catalog on one or two disks.
7. Since there are no daily "trade" newspapers, the popular library press is defined here as those periodicals with large readerships,

such as *LJ Hotline, Library Journal, Wilson Library Bulletin,* and others that appear most frequently: weekly, biweekly, or monthly.

8. MARC is a set of file structures and content designators devised, beginning in the 1960s, by the Library of Congress (LC) for the input, manipulation, and transmission of its bibliographic data by computer. MARC was adopted immediately by the Online Computer Library Center and Utlas, the oldest and largest U.S. and Canadian national bibliographic networks, respectively, and several years later by the younger Research Libraries Information Network and Western Library Network, all of whom used LC's MARC database as a bibliographic source file for their participants.

Despite criticism from experts in the field about its complexity, the MARC standard eventually was adopted by developers of local computer systems intended for individual libraries, too, since the purchasers of these systems wanted to take advantage of their pool of MARC-formatted bibliographic records created using one of the national networks. Even if a library did not participate in a national bibliographic network, commercial sources for computerized data were likely to be available in MARC format, so compatibility with MARC was a distinct asset.

9. James G. Neal, "The Evolving Public/Technical Services Relationship," 111–19.

10. Carlen Ruschoff, "The Year's Work in Descriptive Cataloging, 1989," *Library Resources & Technical Services* 34 (July 1990): 338–49.

11. Jonathan S. Intner, "Beasts in a Box: Choosing Microcomputers for Libraries," in *The Library Microcomputer Environment: Management Issues*, eds. Sheila S. Intner and Jane Anne Hannigan (Phoenix: Oryx Press, 1988), 78.

12. Ibid.

13. Nancy L. Eaton, "Training and Continuing Education for Catalogers: The Electronic Environment of the 1990's," in *Recruiting, Educating, and Training Cataloging Librarians*, 329–39.

CHAPTER 3: ACQUISITIONS AND
COLLECTION MANAGEMENT

1. Association of Research Libraries, Office of University Library Management Studies, Systems and Procedures Exchange Center, *SPEC Flyer, No. 11* (Washington: ARL/OMS, 1974). A study of ninety-three ARL libraries conducted in the early 1980s reported by Sohn concluded that no specific organizational pattern is predominant. Jeanne Sohn, "Collection Development Organizational Patterns in ARL Libraries," *Library Resources & Technical Services* 31 (Apr./June 1987): 123–34.

2. Tauber, *Technical Services in Libraries*, [109].
3. *The Public Library Mission Statement and Its Imperatives for Service* (Chicago: American Library Association/Public Library Association, 1979); *Standards for College Libraries* (Chicago: Association for College and Research Libraries, 1975); *Statement of Quantitative Standards for Two-Year Learning Resources Programs* (Chicago: Association for College and Research Libraries, 1980).
4. Among these are the following: Vernon E. Palmour, et al., *A Planning Process for Public Libraries* (Chicago: American Library Association, 1980); Mary Jo Lynch, *Library Data Collection Handbook* (Chicago: American Library Association, 1981); *User Surveys and Evaluation of Library Services: SPEC Kit #71* (Washington: Association of Research Libraries, 1981).
5. Elizabeth Futas, *Library Acquisitions: Policies and Procedures*, (Phoenix: Oryx Press, 1977).
6. Elizabeth Futas, *Library Acquisitions: Policies and Procedures*, 2d ed. (Phoenix: Oryx Press, 1984) and *Guide to Writing a Bibliographer's Manual* (Chicago: American Library Association/Resources and Technical Services Division, 1989).
7. Although many people believe more always is better, this belief is not universal. Stanley Slote, a library consultant specializing in weeding, claims that having too many undesirable looking items on a shelf buries the desirable ones and lowers the chances that a browser will select any of them, even the desirable ones.
8. David L. Vidor and Elizabeth Futas, "Collection Development in Professional School Collections," (Bethesda, MD: ERIC Document Reproduction Service, ED 276 453, 1986).
9. Bill Katz, "A Way of Looking at Things," *Library Trends* 33 (Winter 1985): 379.
10. William E. McGrath, "Collection Evaluation—Theory and the Search for Structure," *Library Trends* 33 (Winter 1985): 241–66.
11. Allen Kent, et al, *Use of Library Materials: The University of Pittsburgh Study* (New York: Marcel Dekker, 1979).
12. Research Libraries Group, *Conspectus* (Mountain View, CA: RLG, 1985–   ).
13. David Farrell and Jutta Reed-Scott, "The North American Collections Inventory Project: Implications for the Future of Coordinated Management of Research Collections," *Library Resources & Technical Services* 33 (Jan. 1989): 15–28.
14. Elizabeth Futas and David L. Vidor, "Effective Collection Developers: Librarians or Faculty?" *Library Journal* 112 (Apr. 15, 1987): 45–47.

CHAPTER 4: PRESERVATION MANAGEMENT

1. "Guide for Written Collection Policy Statements," Subcommittee on Guidelines for Collection Development, Collection Man-

agement and Development Committee, Resources Section, Resources and Technical Services Division, American Library Association. Bonita Bryant, ed. (Chicago: American Library Association, 1989), 23.

2. George M. Cunha, "The Management of Library Conservation," *Library Lectures*, No. 29–35, Sept. 1974–Apr. 1976 (Baton Rouge, LA: Louisiana State University, 1978), 1–10, and discussed in greater detail in Cunha's other monographs cited in the "Selective Reference Collection" at the end of this chapter.

3. Encapsulation is a simple inexpensive technique by which a document is enclosed between two clear sheets of polyester film so that it can be handled safely. The technique was developed at the Library of Congress and is described in *Polyester Film Encapsulation* (Washington: Library of Congress, 1980).

   Machines that encapsulate documents are available and can be employed to treat large numbers of materials. The cost of such machines is very high—beyond the budgets of medium-sized libraries. However, regional centers that own encapsulation machines, such as the Northeast Document Conservation Center, can provide these services to individual libraries.

4. See *Security for Libraries, People, Buildings, Collections*, ed. Marvine Brand (Chicago: American Library Association, 1984), and current journals, such as *Library and Archival Security* for up-to-date information on the topic.

5. American National Standards Institute, *American National Standard for Information Sciences—Permanence of Paper for Printed Library Materials* (Washington: American National Standards for Information Sciences, 1984). ISSN 8756–0860; Z39.481984.

6. *The Standard for Library Binding*, 8th ed., eds. Paul A. Parisi and Jan Merrill-Oldham (Rochester, NY: Library Binding Institute, 1986); Jan Merrill-Oldham and Paul A. Parisi, *A Guide to the Library Binding Institute Standard for Library Binding* (Chicago: American Library Association, 1990).

7. George M. Cunha, *op. cit.*, 9; reprinted in *Library and Archives Conservation: 1980s and Beyond*, by George Martin Cunha and Dorothy Grant Cunha, vol. 1 (Metuchen, NJ: Scarecrow Press, 1983), 135.

CHAPTER 5: CATALOGING, CLASSIFICATION, AND INDEXING

1. Charles A. Cutter, "Introduction," in *Rules for a Dictionary Catalogue*, 4th ed. (Washington: U.S. Government Printing Office, 1904), 12.

2. In fairness to the member-library contributors of both networks, one must recognize that the errors constitute a very small

proportion of the total data entered as well as the fact that the proportion of errors affecting retrieval is even smaller. A discussion of cataloging quality and errors may be found in Sheila S. Intner, "Quality in Bibliographic Databases: An Analysis of Member-Contributed Cataloging in OCLC and RLIN," in *Advances in Library Administration and Networking*, Gerard McCabe and Bernard Kreisman, eds. vol. 8 (1989): 1–24.

3. Ruth Hafter, *Academic Librarians and Cataloging Networks* (Greenwich, CT: JAI Press, 1986).

4. A comprehensive discussion of the issues may be found in *Recruiting, Educating, and Training Cataloging Librarians* and *Cataloging: The Professional Development Cycle*, eds. Sheila S. Intner and Janet Swan Hill (Westport, CT: Greenwood Press, 1991).

5. Full screen editing, i.e., the capability of making changes in any part of the screen by moving the computer cursor to the place where the desired change is to be made, is not always available to libraries that have no dedicated (i.e., permanently assigned) link to network computers. Libraries without dedicated links usually substitute dial access to network computers, which may only be able to support line editing, i.e., editing just one line of the record at a time.

6. *Searching the Online Union Catalog*, second ed. (Dublin, OH: OCLC, 1982). A pocket-sized pamphlet summarizing available search options is available free upon request from OCLC Inc., 6565 Frantz Road, Dublin, OH 43017. Also useful is Patricia E. Jensen, *Using OCLC: A How-To-Do-It Manual for Libraries* (New York: Neal Schuman Publishers, 1989).

7. Swanson, Gerald L. *Dewey to LC Conversion Tables* (New York: CCM Information Corp., 1972). This is one volume in a three-volume set. The other two volumes include an LC to Dewey conversion table and a listing by LC subject headings that gives both LCC and DDC numbers for each heading.

8. Arlene Taylor Dowell, *Cataloging with Copy: A Decision-Maker's Handbook*, 2d ed. (Littleton, CO: Libraries Unlimited, 1988).

9. James G. Neal, "The Evolving Public/Technical Services Relationship," 111–19; D. Kaye Gapen, "Transition and Change: Technical Services at the Center," *Library Resources & Technical Services* 33 (July 1989): 285–96; and Maureen Sullivan, "On the Job Training: Issues and Answers," in *Cataloging: The Professional Development Cycle*.

CHAPTER 5: DOCUMENT DELIVERY SERVICES: CIRCULATION AND INTERLIBRARY LOANS

1. A history of the conferences, the Universal Bibliographic Control program, and the development of international standards such

as the International Standard Bibliographic Description (ISBD) may be found in *Foundations of Cataloging: A Sourcebook*, eds. Elaine Svenonius and Michael Carpenter (Littleton, CO: Libraries Unlimited, 1985).

2. F. W. Lancaster, *Toward Paperless Information Systems* (New York: Academic Press, 1978); and later, F. W. Lancaster, *Libraries and Librarians in an Age of Electronics* (Arlington, VA: Information Resources Press, 1982).

3. Vannevar Bush, "As We May Think," *Atlantic Monthly* (July 1945): 101–08.

4. Computerized information often is obtained by subscribing to the database(s) of a host computer located far from the library. The library does not receive any physical documents to put on its shelves. Indeed, even when a CD-ROM disk to be used on local computers is provided to the library, if the subscription ends the library must return the disk and is left with nothing, unlike subscriptions to printed materials. For a discussion of the importance of library control over computer-based information resources, see Patricia Battin, "The Library: Centre of the University," *Scholarly Publishing* 17 (Apr. 1986): 255–67.

5. In 1988 Elizabeth Futas warned, "The creation of separate departments for manual and online reference services may indicate a difference between free and fee-based services, but the idea that they are separate functions has developed independent of the decision to charge fees to patrons. In some libraries, the distinction between manual and online tools is perceived as a difference between having real materials and contracting for services from outside sources, not as having the same information in different formats. This may splinter an already divided function even further, creating more confusion for patrons and the possible loss of control over online reference sources. Failing to come to grips with the issues of new technology will create an enormous disservice that may fulfill the gloomy prophecies of the 1970s about the withering away of the library." Elizabeth Futas, "Collection Use: Reference Work with Hardware and Software," in *The Library Microcomputer Environment*, 59. Sheila S. Intner asks: "Is there any truth to the proposition that a librarian can be a librarian without collections? If the 'library' does not own or handle documents that comprise important and heavily used parts of the collection, is it still really a library or does it become merely an information brokerage? Does 'providing access' cease to be a function of libraries and librarians when there are no materials to be purchased, cataloged, and shelved?" "Interfaces: Differences between Access vs. Ownership," *Technicalities* 9 (Sept. 1989): 7.

6. The material in this section is adapted from Sheila S. Intner's

Circulation Policy in Academic, Public, and School Libraries (Westport, CT: Greenwood Press, 1987). The book, a description and analysis of circulation policies in the three types of libraries, is based on findings from a survey of selected libraries conducted by the author in 1983–84. It includes excerpts from policy documents intended for use by staff members and by borrowers in the responding libraries.

7. *Interlibrary Loan Codes, 1980,* American Library Association, Reference and Adult Services Division, Interlibrary Loan Committee, [and] *International Lending Principles and Guidelines, 1978,* International Federation of Library Associations and Institutions, Section on Interlending (Chicago: American Library Association, 1981), 9–11. See also the model code for smaller geographic entities, 6–8.

8. An example is the "Illinois Interlibrary Loan Code," *Illinois Libraries* 71 (Feb. 1989): 140–42.

9. Larger libraries are not always net lenders. When the ILL group includes special libraries or libraries with important special collections, a larger partner with general collections might rely on the resources of the smaller partners for the subjects in which they specialize. Also, being a net lender is not always bad. State or national libraries, which might be the institutions of last resort in ILL systems, may assign a high priority to providing ILL services to their smaller partners.

10. *Interlibrary Loan Codes, 1980,* 7.

11. Ibid.

12. Ibid., 7–8.

13. Ibid., 8.

14. Ibid.

15. Ibid., 9.

16. Ibid., 10–11.

17. Ibid., 11.

18. Ibid., 8, 11.

19. Ching-chih Chen, et al., "The New Concept of Hyperbase and Its Experimentation on the 'First Emperor of China' Videodisc," *Microcomputers for Information Management* 5 (Dec. 1988): 217–46.

CHAPTER 7: COORDINATED COLLECTION DEVELOPMENT

1. Although only RLIN had previously indicated interest in collection comparisons, in 1989 the OCLC network began marketing a collection evaluation product on CD-ROM that combined a list of the holdings of any member library wishing to purchase the product with the holdings of several peer libraries chosen by that member. The disk is used with software that enables

different kinds of collection comparisons to be made. In 1990, WLN announced availability of a similar product. In the future, national networks may function as facilitators of regional or local efforts at coordinated collection development by providing products (and the research and development investments that underlie product development) to support coordinated activities.

2. A good description of the development of the *Conspectus* can be found in Nancy E. Gwinn and Paul H. Mosher, "Coordinating Collection Development: The RLG Conspectus," *College & Research Libraries* 44 (Mar. 1983): 128–40.

3. See Douglas K. Ferguson and K. T. Pollock, "The Library and Information Resources for the Northwest Program," *Interlending & Document Supply* 14 (Jan. 1986): 25–27; and issues of the *Pacific Northwest Collection Assessment Newsletter* (Salem, OR: Oregon State Library Foundation, 1986–   ).

4. A variety of regional and international uses of the *Conspectus* are described by David Farrell and Jutta Reed-Scott in "The North American Collections Inventory Project [NCIP]: Implications for the Future of Coordinated Management of Research Collections," *Library Resources & Technical Services* 33 (Jan. 1989): 15–28. The NCIP, the article's main subject, is one of the largest and best developed of such projects in the research library community.

5. In making this statement, the authors hasten to remind readers that attempts to maintain joint collections physically have been tried in the past and have been met with little success. The costs of maintaining that kind of joint venture may far outweigh its potential benefits, and such costs should be projected conservatively and considered very carefully before the project is undertaken.

Selected Annotated Bibliography

Some useful sources dealing generally with the topic of technical services are cited here. They are not intended to duplicate the references given in the Notes.

Altmann, A. E. "The Academic Library of Tomorrow: Who Will Do What?" *Canadian Library Journal* 45 (June 1988): 147–52.

Challenges the traditional division of public and technical services.

Bloomberg, Marty, and G. Edward Evans. *Introduction to Technical Services for Library Technicians.* 5th ed. Littleton, CO: Libraries Unlimited, 1985.

A widely used text for paraprofessional staff members.

Cargill, Jennifer S. "Budgetary Constraints: The Impact on Technical Services." *Journal of Library Administration* 10, no. 1 (1989): 39–57.

———. "Integrating Public and Technical Services Staffs to Implement the New Mission of Libraries." *Journal of Library Administration* 10, no. 4 (1989): 21–31.

———, ed. "Library Management and Technical Services: The Changing Role of Technical Services in Library Organizations." *Journal of Library Administration* 9 (1988): 1 154.

A special issue with timely contributions on the general topic of

technical service management. Also issued as a separate mono-
graph.

Crawford, Walt. *Technical Standards: An Introduction for Librarians.*
White Plains, NY: Knowledge Industry Publications, 1986. Available from G. K. Hall, Boston, MA.

A basic reference source written in easily understandable language.

Creth, Sheila, and Frederick Duda, eds. *Personnel Administration in
Libraries.* 2d ed. New York: Neal-Schuman Publishers, 1989.

A comprehensible handbook on all aspects of personnel management, including recruitment, legal issues, personnel planning,
staff development, salary administration, performance evaluation,
etc.

Dumont, P. E. "Creativity, Innovation, and Entrepreneurship in
Technical Services." *Journal of Library Administration* 10, no. 2
(1989): 57–68.

Dwyer, James R. "The Evolutionary Role of Technical Services."
Journal of Library Administration 9, no. 1 (1988): 1–13.

Ford, K. E. "Interaction of Public and Technical Services: Collection
Development as Common Ground." *Journal of Library Administration* 9, no. 1 (1988): 13–26.

Godden, Irene P., ed. *Library Technical Services: Operations and Management.* Orlando, FL: Academic Press, 1984.

Contains several useful chapters on various aspects of technical
services, especially automation (by Karen L. Horny), acquisitions
(by Marion T. Reid), and Preservation (by A. Dean Larsen). Some
of the information now is out of date.

Gorman, Michael, ed. *Technical Services Today and Tomorrow.* Englewood, CO: Libraries Unlimited, 1990.

A recent publication with authoritative contributers, aimed primarily at academic research libraries.

Hahn, Harvey. *Technical Services in the Small Library.* Chicago: American Library Association, 1987.

Some useful applications for the medium-sized library.

Library Resources & Technical Services. Chicago: American Library
Association, Association for Library Collections and Technical
Services. Quarterly.

Scholarly journal of ALCTS, a division of ALA, includes reports of
research and other scholarly articles on all aspects of technical
services. Yearly summaries of the literature, divided into five (or

more) broad subtopics in technical services, help in keeping up with a burgeoning body of information. Also helpful is the *ALCTS Newsletter*, which has fewer articles but appears six times a year and includes news of division activities.

Pitkin, Gary M., ed. *Cost-Effective Technical Services: How to Track, Manage, and Justify Internal Operations*. New York: Neal-Schuman Publishers, 1989.

A practical handbook based on a preconference program of the Resources and Technical Services Division (now ALCTS). Focuses on acquisitions and cataloging costs.

Sellen, Betty-Carol, and Betty J. Turock, eds. *The Bottom Line Reader: A Financial Handbook for Librarians*. New York: Neal-Schuman Publishers, 1990.

Selected articles from issues of *The Bottom Line*, a magazine devoted to library finance. Topics include creative budgeting, cost finding, reading financial statements, fundraising, etc.

Shoemaker, Sarah, ed. *Collection Management: Current Issues*. New York: Neal-Schuman Publishers, 1989.

Also issued as a double issue of *Collection Building*. Contributions cover new storage and communication technologies, serials, preservation, evaluation, budgeting, etc.

Simpson, I. S. *Basic Statistics for Librarians*. 3d ed. Chicago: American Library Association, 1988.

A useful tool for all technical services managers.

Stueart, Robert D. *Library Management*. 3d ed. Littleton, CO: Libraries Unlimited, 1987.

A well-established textbook for all librarians involved in management.

————. *Performance Analysis and Appraisal: A How-To-Do-It Manual for Librarians*. New York: Neal-Schuman Publishers, 1990.

A recent very useful publication for staff evaluation.

Technicalities. Lincoln, NE: Media Publications/Westport Publishers. Monthly.

A lively periodical edited by Brian Alley. Includes regular columns on collection development (by Peggy Johnson), indexing (by William Studwell), automation (by David Genaway), and general technical services issues (by Sheila Intner), as well as news, product reviews, and other items of interest to technical services librarians.

Webb, Gisela M. "Strategies for Recruiting Technical Services Personnel." *Technicalities* 8 (Nov. 1988): 13–15.

Weintraub, D. Kathryn. "Shall We Throw Out the Technical Services—and Then What? A LRTS Subsection." *Library Resources & Technical Services* 33 (July 1989): 284–85, and subsequent issues.

A series of articles by D. Kaye Gapen, Liz Bishoff, Lois Kershner, and Joan Rapp intended to provide descriptive detail about changing directions in technical services and ways to implement desired changes. Originally presented at the 1987 annual meeting of the California Library Association Technical Services Chapter.

Wortman, William A. *Collection Management: Background and Principles*. Chicago: American Library Association, 1989. A comprehensive guide to various aspects of collection management.

Index

Academic libraries, xvi, 56, 93–94; in survey, 1–3, 159–60
Access, 102
Acquisitions, xi, xii, xiv–xv, 6, 7, 35–58, 147–49; process, 36; units, 56
Alabama, 1
Alaska, 128
Allocation of funds, 39, 49–50
American Library Association, xviii, 38, 60, 67, 112
American Library Directory, 4
Anderson, Dorothy, 98
Anglo-American Cataloging Rules (AACR), 98; AACR2, 80, 83
Apple computer, 144; Apple II, 31
Approval plans, 48, 49; selection, 44–45
Archives, 140
Arkansas, 1
Artificial intelligence, 146
Association for Libraries and Information Science Education (ALISE), xviii
Association for Library Collections and Technical Services, xviii
Association of Research Libraries, xvi, 36
Audiovisual holdings, 3, 4; materials, 37, 140
Augusta (GA), 2
Australia, 14

Automated systems, 12
Automation, xii, xvii, xix, xx, 17, 141
Avram, Henriette, 99

Baker Library, Harvard University, 41
Baltimore (MD), 2
Baltimore County Public Library, 42
Bar code, 105–6
Bboard services, 118–19
Bibliographic control, xii, 98; data transfer, 21; databases, shared, 125; networks, computerized, 112, 114–15, 116, 123; systems, computerized, 12, integrated, 89–91, linked, 91–92, local enhanced, 90–91; utilities, 75–78, 79, 80, 93, 141, impact on interlibrary loan, 114–15; utility files, 93–94
Bibliographic Retrieval Services (BRS), 91, 99
Bibliographies, 58–59, 70–72, 95–96, 121–22, 138, 181–84
Biological damage, 62
Binding standard, 67
Book cards, 104–5; catalog, 74
Books in Print, 90
Borrowers, categories of, 109
Boston (MA), 2
Boulder (CO), 3

Bowker Company, 90
Brentwood (NY), 3
Bridgeport (CT), 2
Brigham Young University, 19
Bryn Mawr (PA), 3
Budget, 39, 44, 148
Buffalo (NY), 3

California, 1, 14
Canada, 14
Card catalog, 74
Cards, book, 104; library, 105
Catalog interface, 150
Cataloging, xi, xv, 6, 7, 33–34, 73–
94, 150–51; automatic, 150; com-
puterized, 85; deprofessionalism
of, 85–86; distributed, 57–58;
original, 86, 89; staff, 85–86;
tools, 150
Cataloging and Classification Sec-
tion, Research and Technical
Services Division (ALA), xviii
Catalogs, types, 74–75
CD ROM, 15, 31–31, 76, 90, 93, 118,
128, 141, 143, 144, 145, 148; in-
dexes, 148
Chemical deterioration, 62
Chicago, 2
Ching-chih Chen, 118
Circulation, xii, 4, 6, 7, 98, 103, 152;
computerized, 105, 106–7, 108,
110–11; control, 13, 103–8; poli-
cies, 108–11
Classification, 48, 80
Client populations, 37, 38
CLSI, xix, 13, 21, 23, 31, 94
Codes for interlibrary loan, model,
112, 113; national, 112, 113–14
Collection development, coordi-
nated, 123–38; policies, 39, 40;
shared, 148, 153–54
Collection goals, 39
Collection management, 6, 7, 35–58,
147–49
Colorado, 1
Columbia University, xvii, 14
Computer-assisted systems, 12
Computer costs, 13; hardware com-
ponents, 18; laboratory, 30; oper-
ators, working conditions, 25;
workstations, 140
Computer-based catalogs (OPAC),

75, 76; information systems, 102;
materials, 37; networks, 98; order-
ing, 47; systems, advantages, 16;
technical services, 141
Computers, xix, xx
Computing, 10–34; services, 7
Connecticut, 1
Conservation, definition, 6
Conspectus, 43, 126
Conversion, costs, 26; of data, 25–
26, 27; tables (LCC-DCC), 82–83
Coordinated collection develop-
ment, 123–38; data, 132–33; deci-
sions, 129–30; evaluation, 135–36;
implementation, 133–35; struc-
ture, 130–32
Copenhagen, 98
Copy cataloging, 76–77, 81; tools,
81–83
Copyright, 137, 156
Costs, 13, 155; of data conversion,
26
Council on Library Resources, xviii
Cunha, George M., 67
Cutter, Charles A., 74

Dallas (TX), 2
Damage types, 61–62
Data processing, 32
Database management, 7
Dearborn Heights (MI), 3
Descriptive cataloging, standardiza-
tion, 98
Detroit (MI), 3
Dewey Decimal Classification
(DDC), 48, 80, 81, 82, 83
Dialog, 91, 99, 100
Dictionary catalog, 74
Digital electronics, 13
Disaster preparedness, 66
Discards, 64
Distributed processing, 87–88
Document delivery, 97–121, 141,
151–52
DOS windows, 144
DYNIX, 19

East Hartford (CT), 3
East Providence (RI), 3
Eaton, Nancy L., 34
EBSCO, 90

Editing, 78, 81; policy, 83–83; tools, 81–83
Electronic bulletin boards, 118–19; delivery systems, 117; information, 142–43; library, 139–57; publishing, 101–2, 117–18; texts, 100–2
Emergency planning, 66
Emory University, 41, 43
Emperior I project, 118
Environmental control, 64–65, 68
Evaluation, 148; objective, 40–41; of collection, 40, 52; qualitative, 41
Exchanges, 51
Expert systems, 146

Faxon, 90
Federal funding, 11
Fees for service, 155–56
Financial management, 49–50; reports, 56
Fort Worth (TX), 2
Fund accounting, 49, 50
Furnishings, computer, 24–25
Futas, Elizabeth, 40, 41

Gapen, D. Kaye, 88
Gaylord, 93
Gifts, 49–51; and exchanges, 7
Glossary, 161–70
Goals for coordinated collection management, 129–30
Godden, Irene P., xii
Gorman, Michael, xii, xvi
Gorman model, 151
Government documents, 7, 37
Graphical User Interfaces (GUI), 144
Greenway, Ernest, 49

Handling, of materials, 65
Hardware, 13
Hartford (CT), 3
Harvard University, 14, 41
Hattiesburg (MS), 3
Havatny, Bela, 13
Health problems, computer operators, 25
Holistic librarian, 88–89
HVAC (heating, ventilation, air-conditioning) systems, 68
Hypercard, 144–45

IBM, 3; IBM-DOS, 154
Identifiers, standard, 147
Income, library, 4
Indexes, electronic, 100; online, 117
Indexing, 150–51
Indiana, 1, 2
Indiana University, 88
Information brokers, 99; explosion, 11
Integrated systems, 14, 21–22
Interfaces, 22–23
Interlibrary loan, 6, 7, 41–42, 98, 100, 111–116, 121, 123, 143, 152; codes of procedures, 112–14
International Standard Bibliographic Description (ISBD), 98
International Standard Book Numbers (ISBN), 47, 48, 147
International Standards Organization, 21
Intner, Jonathan, 32
Iowa State University, 34
IRVING, 142

Job descriptions, 29

Kansas City (MO), 2
Katz, Bill, 42
Kentucky, 1
Kilgour, Frederick, 13, 99

LEXIS, 142
Library and Information Resources for the Northwest (LIRN), 126, 137
Library associations, 3; cards, 105; conservation, 60–61; networks, 153
Library of Congress, xix, 15, 16, 48, 74, 77, 79, 80, 81, 82, 93, 126, 142; classification (LCC), 80, 81, 82, 83
Linked systems project (LSP), 142
Livermore (CA), 3
Lockheed, 99
Louisiana, 1

Machine readable cataloging. See MARC
MacIntosh (computer), 31, 144, 154
Mainframe computer, 12
Maintenance, building, 65
Manual systems, 10

MARC (machine readable cataloging), xix, 15, 21, 26, 77, 79, 82, 83, 99, 143, 147, 150
Marcive, 93
Maryland, 1
Massachusetts, 63
Materials processing, xii
McGrath, William E., 42
Media production, 10–11
Medium-sized library, xix, definition, ix–x
Methodology, xx–xxi
Microcomputers, 31, 92
Microfilm, 63, 149
Microform, 11, 36, 140, 149, 151
Minicomputers, 32, 92
Minicomputer-based system, 13
Mission statement of library, 38
Mississippi, 1
Modern Language Association, 145

National Library of Canada, 15
National Union Catalog, 92
Natural language processing, 146
Neal, James, 29, 88
Network cataloging, shared, 81
Networks, bibliographic, 75–76, 79, 83, 85, 90–91, 93
New Mexico, 1
New York City, 2, 3
New York Public Library, 14
NEXIS, 142
Niagara Falls (NY), 3
Non-book materials, 37
North Dakota, 1
Northeast Document Conservation Center, 63, 64, 66
Northwestern University, xix, 19, 43
NOTIS, 19, 94

Objectives, 38, 39
OCLC (Ohio College Library Center), 13, 14, 16, 21, 34, 57, 76, 78, 79, 80, 82, 83, 92, 93, 94, 95, 99, 100, 115, 141, 145
Off-site storage, 54
Ohio, 1, 79
Ohio College Library Center. *See* OCLC
Ohio State University, xix
Oklahoma, 1
Online catalog, 142; indexes, 117
Online Public Access Catalog (OPAC), 75, 76, 78

Online Union Catalog (OLUC), 79, 115, 142
On-site storage, 54
Open Systems Interconnection Reference Model (OSI), 21; standard, 142, OSI/x.25, 154
Optical character recognition label, 106
ORBIT, 99
Order slips, 47
Ordering, 46–50
Oregon, 1
Overdues, 107; fines, 109; tracking, 107
Ownership vs access, 102

Paper, for books, 67; records, 11
Paris, 98
Pennsylvania State University, 29
Periodicals, 4
Personnel, 11
Phonetic matching, 146
Photographic services, 10
Physical damage, 61
Population of survey, xix–xx, 1
Pre-order searching, 45–46, 56
Preservation, xii, 140; definition, 60; management, 60–72, 149–50; guidelines, 67–68; planning, 62–67; survey, 66
Preventive preservation, 64–67
Processing, 6, 7
Providence (RI), 2
Public cagalog, 93, 94
Public library, 56, 94; in survey, 3–4, 160
Public Library Mission Statement, 38
Public service librarian, 88, 95
Public services, 35, 36, 43
Public use computers, 30

Rare materials, 51
Records management, 149–50
Recruiting of catalogers, xviii
Reference, 36, 37, 43
Reference and Adult Services Division (ALA), 112
Reformatting, 63
Reorganization, 29
Repair, 63–64
Replacement, 63
Research Libraries Group, 14, 43, 126, 154

Research Libraries Information Network. *See* RLIN
Resource sharing, 78, 123, 152–54, 155
Resources and Technical Services Division (ALA), Cataloging and Classification Section, xviii
Respondents characterized, 4–9
Retrospective conversion (of data), 26, 27, 80; preservation, 62–64
RLIN, 14, 43, 76, 79, 80, 93, 115, 126, 141, 145
Ruschoff, Carlen, 29

Saint Louis (MO), 2
SAN (standard address number), 47, 48, 147
San Francisco, 2, 3
Security, 65
Selection, 43–45, 89, 148
Serials, 6, 7, 36; catalog, 75; units, 56–57
Shared collection development, 153–54
Shelflist catalog, 74
Simmons College Graduate School of Library and Information Science, xviii
Single function systems, 20
Software, 144; vendors, 19
South Bend (IN), 2
South Dakota, 1
Special Interest Group on Technical Services Education, xviii
Staff, 78; working conditions, 25
Staffing, 7–8, 29, 56, 84–86, 94–95, 120
Standard address numbers. *See* SAN
Stanford University, xix, 14
State university libraries in survey, 1–3
Statistics, demographic, 38, 39
Storage, 53–54; procedures, 65
Strategic planning, 124–25
Subdivisions of technical services, 6, 7
Sullivan, Maureen, 88
Survey population, 1
Systems Development Corporation, 99
Systems management, 7

T-slips, 104
Tallahassee (FL), 2
Task Force on Recruiting and Education for Cataloging, xviii
Tauber, Maurice, xi, xiii, xvi, xvii, 10, 36, 46, 49
Taylor, Arlene, 84
TCP/IP, 154
Technical services, definition, xii–xv; administration, xii
Texas, 1
Thesaurus, 146
Thomson Companies, 14
Titles, job, 4–5
Toronto (Canada), 14
Turnkey systems, 17–20; packages, 18–20

United States, 14
United States Book Exchange (USBE), 52
Universal bibliographic control, 91; union catalog, 98
University of Chicago, xix, 145
University of Illinois, 29
University of Pittsburgh, 42
University of Wisconsin, 29; Madison, 88
Use, patterns of, 42
User interfaces, 23–24, 144–45, 146; training for computer systems, 28
Users, 37, 38
UTLAS (University of Toronto Libraries Automated System), 14, 34, 141

Virginia Polytechnic Institute & State University (VTLS), 19
Vidor, David L., 41

Washington, 1
Washington Library Network, 14
Washington State Library, 14
Weeding, 53, 55
Western Library Network. *See* WLN
Wisconsin, 1
WLN, 14, 16, 34, 76, 93, 141
Working conditions of computer operators, 25
Worksheet for catalogers, 82
Workstations, 31–32

Yale University, 14, 29, 88